SOME OF US

SOME OF US

*People who did well
under Thatcher*

JULIAN CRITCHLEY

JOHN MURRAY

© Julian Critchley 1992

First published in 1992
by John Murray (Publishers) Ltd.,
50 Albemarle Street, London W1X 4BD

A catalogue record for this book is available
from the British Library

ISBN 0-7195-4860-8

Typeset in Linotron 11½/14pt Times
by Rowland Phototypesetting Ltd.,
Bury St Edmunds, Suffolk
Printed and bound in Great Britain by
Cambridge University Press

CONTENTS

CONTENTS

8

INTRODUCTION

WHEN THE Thatcher years ended in November 1990, and Margaret, in tears, drove off from Downing Street, it was the end of a revolution. It was called a monetarist revolution, or a free-market revolution, but the lady herself never saw it in merely economic terms. It was a revolution in attitudes of mind. It had been thus from the day that the Tory party chose Margaret as its leader. One of the most celebrated of her gurus, Alfred Sherman – who was very much 'one of us' – put it this way: 'Thatcherism began less as a doctrine than as a mood.'

This book tries to recall something of the mood of the Britain over which Mrs Thatcher presided. It does so by focusing on a handful of people who did well, one way or another, during the Thatcher years. Only some of them were out-and-out Thatcherites. Others might be described as supporters of the Thatcher revolution with reservations. Others, again, were agnostic in terms of Thatcherism, possibly atheist. Some, such as Ken Livingstone, were positively hostile. But their careers are all pointers, in some way, to the spirit of an age.

The question 'What is a Thatcherite?' is harder to answer than many might imagine. Norman Tebbit, surely, is one of nature's Thatcherites; the Tory party has always had its Norman Tebbits, but only in the special circumstances of the 1980s, one suspects, would he have become the party's chairman. Again, do the ranks of the natural Thatcherites include author Jeffrey Archer, or editor Larry Lamb? One can picture both of them rising to the top in any age, but there was something very Eighties about the soaraway success of Lamb's *Sun* and about the multiplication of the Archer paperbacks on the shelves of airport bookstores around the globe. One cannot understand the nature of the Thatcher revolution without pondering why such men achieved success in the way and at the time they did – and pondering, too, how far Lamb's *Sun* and Archer's paperbacks contributed to the success of political Thatcherism. In examining revolutions, cause and effect tend to get mixed up. To appreciate the full ramifications of the roots of a revolution we have to look at more than politics. The archaeologist can tell us much about the history of an era by sifting through the contents of primeval rubbish dumps. To understand the forces at work in the Eighties one finds oneself picking over, for instance, the tawdry leftovers of the Swinging Sixties. One also finds oneself examining the sociology of a grocer's shop in the Grantham of the Thirties.

The rich tapestry of political life is coloured by characters hard to classify. Was Woodrow Wyatt a natural Thatcherite? He is a not unimportant part of the Eighties landscape, although he would have fitted as well into the landscape of Regency England and perhaps of Renaissance Venice. Like a lot of actors on the stage of Mrs Thatcher's Britain, he was a reformed socialist. Socialism had been a knee-jerk reaction to the Conservatism of a father he disliked. Sad biographical details of this kind have to be recalled because they are part of the small change which provides the background to revolutions. Revolutions are carried out by people with fire in their bellies, but the fire may have been sparked off by a wide range of motives.

And it takes a lot of people to bring off a revolution. One of the saddest things about Margaret Thatcher's obvious distress when she was forced out of Downing Street was her inability to come to terms with the fact that life went on without her. She had difficulty in recognizing that much of her strength, as with the leader of any revolution, was simply that she was a spokesman for the unvoiced hopes, fears and prejudices of a large slice of the population. Churchill said, of 1940: 'The nation had a lion's heart, I had the luck to give the roar.' Sometimes Mrs Thatcher gave the impression of believing she was the only lion in the forest.

Many of the foot soldiers of Thatcherism had, like Woodrow Wyatt, been Labour voters. Socialism in early years was a symptom of Thatcherism in middle life. The common strand, quite simply, was an urge to overthrow the established order. Rupert Murdoch was 'Red Rupert' at Oxford. In the 1980s he had an entrée to No. 10. Alfred Sherman, already mentioned, was a Marxist who fought in the Spanish Civil War and thirty-odd years later was midwife at the birth of Thatcherism. That was an extreme case, but Mrs Thatcher could never have carried out her revolution without the aid of many who, a decade earlier, had been voting for Harold Wilson. Harold articulated the frustration that many British voters felt about the calibre of the people running their country. In the Seventies and Eighties, Margaret Thatcher tapped that same frustration. Contempt for the old guard of her party – indeed the old guard in all walks of life – showed through in most of the policy-making in Downing Street in the 1980s.

Revolutions are about change, and about the overturning of privileges. They are about the introduction of new values, or – what can be even more revolutionary – a return to old ways that have gone out of fashion or have ceased to be respectable. As Prime Minister, Margaret Thatcher spoke often of the virtue of 'Victorian values'. Many of them had survived into the 1920s and 1930s in the provincial values of Alderman Roberts of Grantham. He taught her the simple virtues of being British and the difference between right and wrong, between black and white. She could not see why others saw issues, moral or otherwise, in shades of grey. She saw things in terms of virtue and wickedness where others saw political conundrums to which there was no right or wrong answer. She resented it bitterly when she did not find the moral backing she thought she deserved from the Established Church. Her preferred choice for Archbishop of Canterbury, so the wags said, would really have been Chief Rabbi Jakobovits, who finds an honoured place in these pages. It was no coincidence that Jewish people were well represented in the Thatcher entourage: a new mood, new men. The Established Church was tarred with the same brush as the old establishment of the Tory party.

Thatcherism came into being in the aftermath of the cynical Sixties and like all revolutions was a reaction to what had gone before. The morality of the Grantham grocer's shop included some simple rules which she sought to translate into principles of political action:

Privileges ought to be earned, not awarded on the basis of an old boy network or on the basis that things have always been done like that.

When a privilege has been earned, it is outrageous for anyone else, including the tax collector, to take it away.

Books are there to be balanced, and debt is sinful.

The family is the unit of society, and ideally all social welfare should be a family responsibility.

Since individuals are responsible for their individual failure, it is pointless for 'society' to feel guilty; and much bad government and many bad laws have resulted from trying to assuage collective guilt – guilt about unemployment, about colonialism, about homelessness, about racial prejudice and so on.

It was a political philosophy so obvious to Margaret Thatcher's mind that she was convinced the ordinary British citizen was entitled to feel righteous anger at the way he had been cheated over the past century by his rulers, by the bumbling of ruling classes too stupid, or too morally lazy, to observe those simple rules.

The virtue of that homespun philosophy comes through in some of the character sketches in this volume, but not by any means in all of them. There are success stories here indeed of the fruits of hard work and of virtue rewarded. But the Thatcher years saw many, many success stories where the simple virtues were less evident. If Thatcherism was not altogether about monetarism, it is certainly true that much of the new spirit of the age was about money. The heyday of the Thatcher years was the period of 'Big Bang' in the City. Young men and women who would not have been high up in the pecking order of the old Britain were earning, or at least were receiving, salaries measured in telephone numbers. Some of them were not nice people. If it was desirable to see new men emerging, it was less pleasing to see a new brashness, and a new cynicism exceeding anything from the Harold Wilson years. It is hard to imagine that the grocer of Grantham would have approved. He would not have liked the antics of the takeover merchants of the City in the late 1980s, or the sight of a credit-hungry consumer society set on getting its wants satisfied now, to be paid for later.

Of course, money was often the measure of real achievement. These were the years of the 'enterprise society' that produced a new breed of entrepreneurial businessman. It was the time when many of the more enterprising managers who had been locked into the typical corporate structure of the more lackadaisical areas of British industry, earning comfortable salaries in the hierarchy of the big companies, were moved to take themselves off to found their own businesses. Part of the motivation, but usually not all of it, was the prospect of what in the language of the times was called 'serious money'. Many of them achieved just that, when their businesses were in due course floated on the new Unlisted Securities Market which became one of the monuments of the Thatcher years.

No harm in that, of course. These new entrepreneurs – the 'USM millionaires' – were showing initiative all too often lacking in the traditional British business world of the Sixties and Seventies. This book includes a couple of the more interesting of the successful entrepreneurs of the Thatcher years, Anita Roddick of Body Shop, and Tim Waterstone of Waterstone's. Both combined great business acumen with high moral principles. But niceness is not invariably part of the character of the successful man or woman. You cannot – this was part of the accepted wisdom of the Thatcher years – make an omelette without breaking eggs. Unfortunately, one of the uglier developments was an increasing assumption that the mere act of breaking eggs inevitably results in the making of an omelette. The merely macho became confused, too often, with what was bold and courageous.

Authority and power were very much part of the Thatcher style of government, and the same spirit came to the fore in other departments of British life. In one of the essays collected under the title *Thatcherism* (Chatto, 1988), edited by Robert Skidelsky, David Marquand writes: 'Thatcherism is a sort of British Gaullism . . . Like Gaullism, it was born out of a growing sense of despair . . . A generation of political decline seemed to have led to a crisis of governability.'

The importance of seizing the reins of power – and then hanging grimly on to them – came through in the Westland episode which forms part of this story, and indeed in the strange phenomenon of Bernard Ingham's tenure of office at No. 10. The centralization of power often contrasted oddly with the free-market philosophy which was another main strand of Thatcherism. Economic liberalism means that the man from Whitehall does not know best. Yet the Thatcher years saw a substantial accretion of power to Whitehall. It was rather like the paradox of Marxism – Communists talking of the withering away of the State while building up the power base of the Kremlin. The Thatcher government took away much of the power of the local authorities and brought it to Whitehall. This was to counter the antics of the Loony Left in some London boroughs and in places like Liverpool. But it was not just Loony Leftists who came into conflict with central government. In the Tory shires, solid Conservative councillors resented, for instance, central policies to allow more house-building on green-belt land.

In education policy, the Thatcher government started with a strong penchant for introducing vouchers – the privatization of schooling. Eventually it was decided – by the great privatizer, Keith Joseph, no less – that vouchers were simply not on. Instead, he took more power into his own hands as Education Secretary to raise education standards. The Education Department at the end of the Thatcher years had more power over the content of education, from nursery to university, than it had ever had before. In a famous interview shortly before she became Prime Minister, Margaret Thatcher said of her way of running things: 'It must be a conviction Government. We've got to go in an agreed and clear direction. As Prime Minister I couldn't waste time having any internal arguments.' This explains, among other things, why she became so irritated by the eternal arguments of the European Community. She had difficulty in thinking herself into the world of compromise.

Determination pays political dividends, which is not inconsistent with the fact that opinion polls during the 1980s often showed the Prime Minister to be personally unpopular, although she was able to win three general elections. Electorates sometimes act like schoolboys who may be terrified of old So-and-So the maths master but who would freely admit that he is a better teacher – or, at least, he is better at getting them through exams – than the popular masters in the school.

If there is a moral in this book, it is about the complexity of the forces at work in the Britain of Margaret Thatcher, the only British Prime Minister who has given her name to an 'ism'. That complexity is seen particularly in the difficulties in classifying people as being 'Left' or 'Right'. Mrs Thatcher, accused so often of polarizing people, succeeded in blurring boundaries there. She herself might have said it merely proved the validity of Thatcherite tenets about the plurality of society. The final profit-and-loss account of the Thatcher years will be some time in appearing.

1

An ordinary bloke

JOHN MAJOR

THE THATCHER years were the time when it seemed much easier to make money out of money rather than by making things. The City saw Big Bang – and then Black Monday. There were fewer jobs created during the 1980s among the horny-handed than among the yuppies in evidence in the watering holes of the Square Mile.

Yet the worlds of banking and finance were not exactly natural Thatcherite territory. Bankers did not loom large in the entourage that Margaret built up after taking over from Ted Heath in 1975. According to the demonology of Thatcherites, much of the mess Ted left behind him had been caused by the excesses of secondary banking during his government of 1970–4. So when the Thatcher government came to power, nobody paid much attention to the 36-year-old banker who turned up in the 1979 crop of new Tory MPs. In fact there was an interesting link between John Major, Associate of the Institute of Banking, and the Heath regime. He had worked at the Standard Chartered Bank with its chairman Lord Barber who, as Tony Barber, had been Ted's Chancellor of the Exchequer and whose 'Barber Boom' had been responsible for much of the inflation that the 1979 Thatcher government was determined to squeeze out of the system.

How true a Thatcherite is John Major? We know that some time in the late 1980s, when he had been an MP for less than ten years, Margaret seems to have earmarked him as a possible successor, although clearly she was thinking of a very distant point in time. We know that when she did indeed step down so unwillingly, she campaigned for him with characteristically vigorous partisanship. We know also that within a matter of weeks she was bitterly regretting, intermittently, that she had allowed the garment of leadership to be snatched from her.

There was a double irony – some would say a double poetic justice – in the manner of her departure. There were uncanny similarities between the way she won the leadership and the way she lost it. On both occasions it was a relatively inexperienced member of the party who emerged unexpectedly, and late in the day, as victor. And on both occasions the result followed determined efforts by a skilful group of right-wingers to get the result they wanted for the party.

The other irony was that Margaret Thatcher, whose hallmark had been a *style* more than a philosophy of government, should have been ousted by someone whose style was so different, almost ludicrously different. Confrontation suddenly gave way to consensus, one-person government to government by Cabinet debate, aggressive self-assurance to modesty. Instead of a crusade, with enemies to be vanquished, national leadership became something to be settled quietly and sensibly round a boardroom table.

Of course there were other ways in which John Major was a very natural successor to Margaret. This was no return to the upper-class and paternalistic traditions which, pre-Thatcher, had set the tone of British public life for the greater part of the twentieth century. John Major launched his Premiership with a message of meritocracy: he believed in the 'classless society'.

Margaret had come from solid shopkeeping stock. As became well known from scores of profiles written at the time of her resignation, John's background was more colourful. His father was a man whose entrepreneurial instincts were rather different from those of Alderman Roberts of Grantham. A one-time trapeze artist, and for a time a professional baseball player in America, the elder Major was in his mid-sixties when John was born. During the boy's childhood his latest business venture (making garden gnomes) took a turn for the worse. The family had to move from the Surrey suburbs into two rooms in Brixton.

Brixton provided the young Major with a context for his social philosophy. It also provided him with the opportunity – and being a nice man he may well have thought this was more important – to watch cricket at the Oval. Old-fashioned Tories used to like to use cricketing metaphors. Relatively few modern Tories actually take the game seriously, but John is one of them. There is a rather typical Jeffrey Archer story about going to Lord's with John when he had recently been promoted to the Cabinet and noticing the legendary Len Hutton in the MCC president's box. Jeffrey knew Hutton. John didn't and was delighted to be introduced.

Later Jeffrey encountered John's son James at a party and asked him whether his father had ever mentioned having met Hutton. 'Yes,' said the boy, 'daily.'

But it was not all cricket at the Oval. It was necessary, as other anecdotes duly noted, for the young John Major to earn a living in the Brixton days. He was a trainee accountant but didn't like it. He tried and failed to get on the buses (he didn't pass the physical agility test). He did labouring jobs. He had a spell with the Electricity Board at the Elephant and Castle. There were also spells on the dole. 'I used to go job-hunting in the morning and when that came to naught, as it did come to naught, I trotted off to the pictures for a shilling in the afternoon.' Eventually he settled for banking.

What didn't come to naught were his early political activities. The story is that his first visit to the House of Commons was when he was conducted round by the colourful local (Labour) MP, Colonel Marcus Lipton. If he had been a typical Thatcherite he would no doubt have joined the Labour party and had a road-to-Damascus conversion. But he was content to work his passage locally on behalf of the Heath-led party. The famous soap box was used to take the message to the streets. Opportunities for trotting off to the pictures in the afternoon presumably became much fewer.

Banking took him to Nigeria (at the height of the Biafra fighting). He came home crippled as a result of a road accident, and there followed the famous period in a Croydon hospital when he came to respect the National Health Service. He read Agatha Christie, Trollope (like Harold Macmillan) and cricket books.

South London provided his political apprenticeship. That might have turned him into one of the less likeable Tory local politicians. In fact the evidence is that on the Lambeth council, where he was housing chairman, he really believed that the job of a housing committee was to provide houses for people who needed them. Certainly his near-contemporary Ken Livingstone, watching with some admiration from the other side, seems to have decided that he was a much more effective local politician than the old guard who ran the London Labour party at that time. There is also evidence that South London impressed on him the need for the Conservative party to be colour blind.

A Thatcherite? This was the time when the intellectual high ground of the party was being steadily occupied by the monetarists, and John Major accepted the monetarist argument. He became an MP in the same election which carried Mrs Thatcher into 10 Downing Street.

In the 1979 Parliament, there were really only two kinds of

back-bencher who caught the public imagination. On the one hand were those who set out to show they were more Thatcherite than Thatcher and shouted monetarism to high heaven. On the other hand there were those who had Doubts, and dared to voice them. John Major was in neither camp, and it is not unfair to say he never excited the public at all. He was no monetarist ranter but nor was there any evidence of Doubts. In this he resembled a decent, cricket-playing curate who doesn't argue about theology but knows that his job is to face the world with a straight bat and a stiff upper lip.

In his maiden speech (delivered, significantly, in the debate on the very first Thatcher budget), John established a workmanlike, downbeat style. He said public opinion required four things of the new government: the first two were to cut taxes and to conquer inflation; on that basis it would be possible to achieve the third and fourth – to create new jobs 'and, as far as possible, to maintain satisfactory public services'.

He did not star as a debater, partly because, early on, he accepted the self-denying ordinance of reticence involved in agreeing to be a parliamentary private secretary. Then he was picked for the equally reticent role of a Whip. By 1984 he was a senior Whip, only just turned 40 and rising smoothly up the greasy pole. As all realists at Westminster know, the ultimate power-brokers in British politics are not the flamboyant figures who posture at Question Time or appear on the TV chat shows. The real power rests largely with men in grey suits of whom the TV watchers have never heard.

But then, for a couple of years, John did find himself in front of the cameras when he was promoted to departmental duties at Health and Social Security. It happened to be a particularly bad winter and he was in the firing line over the apparently harsh rules for cold weather payments. In the end, he emerged with a reputation for having reached a compassionate solution. Even more important from the point of view of ascent up the greasy pole, he established himself as a master of the hideous intricacies of the financial structure of the welfare state.

In any event, around this time Margaret Thatcher evidently decided that he was One of Us. At Health and Social Security he had demonstrated that he believed in getting value for the taxpayer's money. She also saw him as one of the best of Us at putting over the Thatcherite philosophy: that the prosaic, straightforward Major style was an excellent foil to the likes of Norman Tebbit. He was selected for an important presentational role in the 1987 election. Immediately after that election came promotion to the Cabinet. This made John the first of the 1979 intake of MPs to reach Cabinet rank – the first Cabinet minister completely innocent of parliamentary politics under a non-Thatcherite Prime Minister. After eight years of Thatcherism, the Prime Minister at last had one colleague in the Cabinet who came to the job, so to speak, squeaky clean.

His Cabinet job – Chief Secretary to the Treasury – took him back to grey-suit politics. Chief Secretaries don't say very much in public. They just hold the purse-strings – the equivalent of holding the power of political life and death over their colleagues. No one, it was said, had ever said No with greater courtesy. The Major style was emerging. 'I do not like personality politics,' he was quoted as saying. 'If Disraeli had been on television, I'm sure he would have come across as a very slippery person. Gladstone might not have been much better. And', he added rather mysteriously, 'what if Lord Palmerston took his teeth out? I prefer people to be judged on what they do.' As Financial Secretary he developed the habit of lunching – egg, sausage and chips – at a suitably modest café round the corner from the Treasury.

Among his less well-known duties at this time was that of keeping the No. 10 press secretary, Bernard Ingham, informed about what went on in Cabinet. After illness forced Willie Whitelaw to retire it was John, according to Ingham, in his memoirs *Kill the Messenger*, who became his 'mentor'.

'He briefed me regularly and thoroughly after Cabinet meetings and gave me a strong and confident base on which to operate with journalists, especially in the economic and social fields.'

He carried out two rounds of the annual expenditure negotiations which provide the parameters of government policy for the next twelve months. Chief Secretaries are not the best-loved people in government, yet expressions of admiration flowed in. He was performing the same kind of balancing act, so said the wits, that his father had shown on the trapeze. Simpler souls merely noted that he was proving that you could be a Thatcherite and a thoroughly nice person. But the most memorable comment at this stage in his career came from an unusual source of compliments. Norman Tebbit, who was then party chairman, said that John was just the sort of 'ordinary bloke' who might take over as Conservative leader after the departure of Herself. Lesser men than John Major might have cringed. For Norman to play kingmaker was rather like the Demon King going around backstage at a pantomime tipping the most competent member of the pantomime chorus line for the next principal boy. Within a week most people had forgotten Norman's remarks, but on the Thatcherite wing of the party there were those who noted what had been said, and put secret marks on their cards.

The succession then seemed a matter of only theoretical interest. But things were moving fast. For reasons for which the Chief Secretary could not be held wholly responsible, the economy was beginning to go badly wrong. Inflation, which was supposed to have been 'squeezed out of the system', was back with us. The political magic of the Thatcher years was beginning to look jaded too. The Thatcher method of government by handbag-swiping was about to rebound on the swiper.

In July 1989 the Prime Minister sought to revive her fortunes, as many Prime Ministers before her have done, by purging her Cabinet. Her way of doing this spoke volumes about the personal style in which the country was being ruled. The key to the changes was the demotion of Geoffrey Howe who, next to Herself, had done most to lay the foundations of Thatcherism when he was Chancellor. Now he was Foreign Secretary, but stood accused of having 'gone native' at the Foreign Office on European issues. He had to go. He was given the title of Deputy Prime Minister but the world was told, in classic Bernard Ingham fashion, that of course the title did not mean much. John replaced him at the Foreign Office. Eyebrows were raised. When Norma Major was telephoned by her husband with the news, she refused to believe him. 'You're winding me up,' she said. She was not the only one to be astonished.

It was scarcely a promotion in ideal circumstances. The good news for John – loudly proclaimed by the media at the time – was that he was obviously being picked as a front runner for the (still distant) succession. The bad news was that the Prime Minister, having sacked Geoffrey for independence of mind, was effectively branding John Major as a man who would do what he was told. Inevitably, there were cynical smiles when the new Foreign Secretary and his political mistress went off to a Commonwealth conference and she gave one of her familiar bravura Commonwealth performances – she allowed her Foreign Secretary to thrash out a balanced joint statement with his opposite numbers in the Commonwealth countries and then publicly distanced herself from it.

All in all, he scarcely had the time to make his mark at the Foreign Office. The Westminster roundabout was now moving even faster. Within a few months the Chancellor, Nigel Lawson, deciding that he had had enough of interference from No. 10 in the business of No. 11 Downing Street, resigned. In a matter of minutes Nigel had been replaced by an heir apparent, John Major.

He had a year as Chancellor – the last of the Thatcher years. With hindsight that year can be seen as a sort of interregnum, and what happened at the end of it had the logic of

a Greek tragedy. It seems astonishing that Margaret did not
see the weakness of her position, until one remembers that
the principal characteristic of the Thatcher years was a forthright refusal to accept anything that the rest of the world
regarded as logic. As the 1980s ended, it was clear to the
rest of the world that the Thatcher government was losing
credibility. After a decade of the application, more or less,
of Thatcherite economic policies, the economy was in trouble
yet again. The non-economic attractions of Thatcherism, like
the assertion of British interests against hostile foreigners,
were jaded.

The Conservative party, which for a decade had been
debating the merits and demerits of Thatcherism, found it
was debating a much earthier topic: if it wanted to ensure yet
another Conservative election victory, which leader would
give it the best chance? Not so long before, the bulk of Conservatives – whether Thatcherite, anti-Thatcherite, neo-
Thatcherite or whatever – would have had little difficulty in
saying that in electoral terms their best hope still lay in Mrs
Thatcher. The number saying that now was diminishing
rapidly – perhaps even more rapidly among the Thatcherites
than among others. The unthinkable was happening – the
possibility that the best way to protect Thatcherism might be
to get rid of the lady herself.

It was a situation which immensely strengthened John
Major's position as the heir apparent, although it took time
for this fact to sink in. Indeed, it does not seem to have
occurred to Margaret at all until she found herself in involun-
tary retirement. John himself was not a man to exploit his
advantage, until circumstances made it impossible for him
to decline the nomination. 'Well,' he remarked to his first
Cabinet, 'who would have believed it?'

The topic that precipitated Margaret's downfall was, ironically, Europe. She had been at odds with so many of her
ministers over British relations with the European Community, always confident – no doubt rightly – that the bulk

of voters shared her anti-European prejudices. She had quar-
relled with Michael Heseltine over a European issue and he
had walked out. It was largely over the European Exchange
Rate Mechanism that Nigel Lawson resigned – the same issue
which had got Geoffrey into trouble. Appropriately it was
Geoffrey who finally blew the whistle, by making a speech
condemning the Thatcher approach to Europe in the most
devastating terms. Equally appropriately it was Michael who
precipitated a leadership election, eventually providing the
parliamentary party with a choice of three candidates; Heseltine, Major and Douglas Hurd.

Why did the victory go to Major? He got the vote of those
who felt it was important to have youth on the Tories' side.
(At the age of 47, he was the youngest Prime Minister since
Lord Rosebery in 1894.) He probably got the 'safety first'
vote, never to be ignored in the Tory party, a large part of
which has always hankered after the days of Stanley Baldwin.
He got at least part of the 'one nation' vote, although each
of the other candidates could put forward a strong case for
that. Thanks to Margaret's endorsement he presumably got
the Little Englander vote, from MPs who within a few weeks
were wondering what had hit them when the new Prime Minister began to make very European noises. The votes he did
not get were from those who felt there was a need for more
experience or who wanted a bit more excitement from a
leader.

What about the Thatcherite vote? We must assume it went
to him. As Rab Butler might have phrased it, he was the best
Thatcherite we'd got. Perhaps there would have been a more
full-blooded Thatcherite candidate on the list if Margaret had
been able to contemplate, in time, that one was needed. But
the fact that there was no clearer successor said something
about the transience of what had once seemed indestructible.

If electability was what his colleagues were looking for
when they chose Major, they had anxious months ahead of
them. It seemed, for long, nail-biting weeks, that he had

fallen down on what is arguably the most important personal decision a Prime Minister has to take – choosing the date of a general election. If he had gone to the country immediately after the Gulf crisis (which had begun in Margaret's time and which John, when he took over, handled with a sure touch), he would have entered the campaign with a head start in the opinion polls. The same would probably have been true if he had gone in the autumn of 1991 when it seemed – a false dawn, as it emerged – that the recession had bottomed out.

Instead he waited until the spring of 1992. The economic indicators slid unhappily towards the bottom of the graph. Unemployment mounted. Week after week, members of the property-owning democracy were having their houses repossessed by building societies. It was not the kind of situation that shows the Conservative party at its best. On the fringes of the party, among the unreconstructed Thatcherite ultras, there were those who made it clear that they would not be unduly sad if John was heading for defeat: it would be a matter of going back to the drawing-board, as in 1974 when the chaos following Ted's double defeat at the polls led to the emergence of Mrs T.

Major's victory of April 1992, against that background, was all the more triumphant. He was now, in the words much used at the time, his own man. This was so obvious that Margaret's unfortunate remarks after the results came through – to the effect that it all just proved the continuity of Thatcherism – seemed to cast further doubt on her judgement.

2

The common touch

NORMAN TEBBIT

NORMAN TEBBIT was arguably the politician who, of his generation, had the greatest rapport with that mythical man in the Clapham omnibus. His classic advice to the unemployed to 'get on their bikes' and find a job rang true to millions of British voters of all social classes. But there was more to it than that. The earthy, brutal way in which Norman said those things was deliberate. He saw it as his duty to slap down the assumptions of a generation reared on woolly idealism, on the notion that 'we are all guilty' if people are unemployed, or if they riot in the streets, or if they feel discriminated against. In other words he rejected, without apology, the post-war consensus whereby both main parties for years accepted governmental responsibility for social ills: he was the rude child saying that the emperor had no clothes. He didn't just say it, he shouted it from the rooftops, jeering at those who pretended to see the clothes.

If Tebbit had entered politics a decade earlier, the Conservative party would have been embarrassed by him. To the Thatcherites he was a hero, if not always the easiest man to get on with. His was the wisdom of the saloon bar transported to the corridors of power. Or at least the wisdom of saloon bars patronized by those who were employed, who were not members of minority groups, who were reasonably good at managing their personal finances and who lived largely in the south-east of the country.

Norman Tebbit's background was lower-middle-class north-east London suburbia. (His constituency was in Essex, in east London suburbia.) He never aped the manners or style of speech that make for the difference between the Essex and the Surrey suburbs. The Tebbit family knew about the toughness of the high unemployment of the 1930s, and his father did indeed get on his bike to look for work. The boy got to a grammar school, and as a national serviceman was commissioned in the RAF and qualified as a pilot.

Norman's civil career started on the fringes of journalism and in advertising: he was a 'boy' in the *Financial Times* office and quickly sensed that there was little future in that environment, where the plum jobs went to confident young men from the right universities who could find their way around the City. The point was not lost on him: he had to fight his way up using the weapons he had been born with.

As an ex-RAF pilot he qualified as a BOAC pilot: the steadiness of nerve required there was no bad training for politics. He had in fact worked for the Conservative party since he was a teenager, but his introduction to public life really came (as did Ronald Reagan's) as an office holder in a middle-class union: in Reagan's case it was the Screen Actors' Guild; in Tebbit's it was the pilots' association, BALPA. He was not popular with the bureaucrats of BOAC.

Norman was soon to become the scourge of the British trade union movement. But he was in tune with people who were once automatically trade union members. He was, you might say, the post-trade-union voice of the British working man. That was what ultimately gave him his power base in the electorate. For years, most politicians, Labour and Tory, had failed to notice, or had averted their eyes from, what was happening among the electors whom the sociologists call the C2s. Harold Macmillan, back in the Fifties, had pointed out that 'most of our people have never had it so good', and had never been forgiven for it. Norman Tebbit looked at the working-class shoppers wheeling their laden trollies to the boots of their cars in the supermarket car parks and knew that here were Tory votes, if you went after them in the right way.

Of course the political mileage did not extend to enthusiasm for the politics of helping the Third World, or being over-generous to immigrants, or handing out large-scale welfare benefits. The Tebbit political constituency consisted of people who were prepared to work hard to swell their pay packets but did not see why a benevolent government should claw back their earnings through PAYE to spread the national wealth around.

Tebbit entered Parliament in 1970, at the start of the Heath government, but disliked various elements of Heath policy, such as that on prices and incomes. It was when Margaret Thatcher ousted Ted Heath as party leader, after the Tories had been defeated in two general elections in quick succession in 1974, that Tebbit became a major Commons figure.

The Tories were in an uneasy state. They are never at their best in opposition, and their policy was in flux, to say the least. As the Gentlemen's Party they were at a particular disadvantage when faced with an infighter like Harold Wilson. So there was a vacuum on the Opposition side, and into it Norman advanced with a sure step. He did not suffer from gentlemanly inhibitions. He could take on, and score points off, even that wily old parliamentary opponent Michael Foot (who dubbed Tebbit 'a semi-house-trained polecat').

He took up the cause of employees penalized by the closed shop beloved of the trade union establishment: 'The voice and common sense of the mass of ordinary British workers will be drowned by the carefully orchestrated shouts of the destructive, hateful doctrines of the red fascists who have seized control of our trade union movement.' Red fascists indeed! This was solar-plexus-pounding stuff for the Labour party.

His style grieved some old-fashioned Tories: newcomers to the party were simply delighted that he so obviously drew blood. When Margaret Thatcher took over as Leader of the Opposition he was a natural part of her praetorian guard. Not only Labour but also the Tory wets had reason to fear his tongue. When she became Prime Minister he rose up the ministerial hierarchy.

When he joined the Cabinet as Employment Secretary in 1981 it seemed that at last the unions were going to be clobbered. He did indeed toughen the laws on strikes, but in one sense it was an anti-climax, because union militancy had already been largely tamed: the grim unemployment figures of the early Thatcher years had seen to that. Then in 1985 Norman took over what seemed to be the natural job for him, when Margaret chose him as chairman of the party: he was to be the man who would, so to speak, wring out the last of Tory wetness. In fact he was not an ideal chairman. Even in a Thatcherite Tory party, the post calls for a lightness of touch which he did not possess. And ironically, when the 1987 election came along, those natural allies, Thatcher and Tebbit, found themselves on opposite sides on an important matter of tactics.

There was a frankness to the Tebbit logic which appealed to many, although not all. It was a logic which formed part, an electorally important part, of the philosophy of the Thatcher years, reaching a high point in the evolution of what became widely known – thanks largely to a piece I wrote in *You*, the *Mail on Sunday*'s glossy magazine – as Essex Man. Essex Man, reader of the *Sun*, scourge of the social security scrounger, and Little Englander, was vital in keeping the Thatcher revolution on the road through the 1980s. The Essex constituencies of the east London hinterland became a Thatcher heartland, with the dominant ethos provided by upwardly mobile *émigrés* from the East End who tended to take with them the bolshie but deeply conservative instincts of the Cockney.

What was true of Essex was true of similar housing-estate Tory heartlands of the West Midlands and elsewhere where the political map had changed from red to blue at the 1979 election. These new Tory voters were first-generation owner-occupiers. They were Thatcherites, and if they had to name a Thatcher-substitute it would probably have been Norman Tebbit, that natural Earl of Essex.

Norman (who was to entitle his memoirs *Upwardly Mobile*) had no pretensions about dictating how the working classes should spend their money in improving themselves. Why shouldn't they buy the *Sun* and enjoy page three? So far as he was concerned it was the equivalent of the precious middle classes going to art galleries and enjoying aesthetically sancti-fied nudity, except that the middle-class aesthete expected the taxpayer to subsidize his pleasure.

A feature of Essex Man (and of the associated species, identi-fied later, Essex Girl) was forthright acknowledgement of the legitimate pleasures of the flesh. Norman Tebbit was no prude. Those who knew Tebbit the politician only from the media pictures of him – the grim, death's-head face, the voice of doom, the stern admonitory finger – often thought of him as an austere, puritanical figure. The evidence is that in his flying days he was very much one of the boys, which is all to his credit. It was apparently a time of noisy, jolly, boozy nights out when he had time off – which did not prevent Norman the pilot from also being a busy, enthusiastic Tory party worker, making his way up the party hierarchy in the outer suburbs of north London.

The story of the rise and fall of Norman Tebbit in the world of Margaret Thatcher is an illustration of a much wider problem that overhung all but the earliest of the Thatcher years: who would succeed her? In the mid-Eighties Norman, strange as it may appear in retrospect, seemed the likeliest candidate. His qualifications as ministerial material were not patently obvious. (Ted Heath once said that *he* would never have given Norman a job at all.) But that deficiency, in the atmosphere of the middle Thatcher years, seems to have been offset in the Leader's eyes by the merit of being so obviously One of Us, his aggressively sound views on the villainy of the trade unions and his admirable contempt for the Old Etonian wing of the party. Nor was the special relationship with the new Tory C2s to be ignored.

It is tempting to say that his Thatcherite credentials made him almost *plus royale que la reine*. That, indeed, was the trouble, as *la reine* was about to find out. As party chairman Norman did not confine himself to organizing and exhorting. He became a Thinker. Thatcherism had been in place now for half a decade – he wanted to move it on as a philosophy and a way of life. This was to commit the cardinal sin of assuming that Thatcherism was something separate from Thatcher. Norman had touched on the heart of the successor problem. (Cecil Parkinson, equally ambitious, but knowing more, perhaps, about the female mind, was more tactful.)

The unhappy episode of Norman as chairman came to a head during the 1987 campaign, but the trouble had become obvious during the previous year when he produced research from Saatchi & Saatchi indicating that the electorate, while still largely Conservative, perceived the current party leadership as being harsh and uncaring. The Prime Minister was less than pleased.

She dealt with the situation in characteristic fashion by bringing in a rival advertising agency who came up with more palatable research. The duality of the party advertising strategy continued through the campaign, and there was added duality when she arranged for Lord Young to shadow the party chairman. The Tebbit chairmanship had not been an unqualified success.

Tebbit did not last long in government after the 1987 election. He had various attractive offers from the private sector. Like Dick Whittington, he turned again and made for the

City. Retirement from politics made sense, too, after his appalling experience in the Brighton bombing, which seriously injured him and left his wife tragically crippled.

He was still a major political figure, though, and the departure of Margaret Thatcher from Downing Street in 1990 presented him in a sense with his greatest opportunity to show his own kind of loyalty to Thatcherism. She left behind much unfinished business in the EEC, culminating in the Maastricht negotiations where the next stage of European unity was thrashed out. One could almost see Margaret's fingers itching to get at the Maastricht issues. But she clearly had not come to any kind of terms with the reality of her new position and the limitations on her scope for action. Norman, whose Little England qualifications were even more impeccable than hers, had no such difficulties. He developed for a time into a sort of leader of the opposition on European unity.

His attitude to the post-Thatcher Tory party was rather like Churchill's description of his relationship with the Church of England: like a flying buttress, Winston said, he supported it from the outside. When the 1992 election came he would not have been the old Norman if he had not felt that the party needed him more than he needed it. Was it his support that carried the day in Essex, where Labour had hoped to win back some of those C2 seats? Norman was entitled to one of his sly smiles when the Essex results came through. Essex Man had, on the whole, stayed firm.

3

The 'nearly' man

CECIL PARKINSON

IF NORMAN was the abrasive face of Thatcherism, Cecil was its smooth face. Each man was seriously perceived for a time as the most likely successor to Margaret Thatcher. The two men had a great deal in common, apart from the purity of their political doctrine, and together their personalities tell us a lot about the spirit of the Thatcher years.

Almost precisely the same age, Cecil Parkinson and Norman Tebbit got to know each other when serving their political apprenticeships in the same corner of the outer London Tory circuit. According to one engaging story, when Cecil was in the chair it was Norman's job to sit at the back of the hall and heckle him if the meeting turned out to be too docile. Both men spoke on the platforms of Home Counties suburbia in accents that would have fascinated Professor Higgins. While Norman was your genuine, south-of-Watford man, Cecil was a Northerner, although never 'Ee ba goom', as he once explained defensively to an interviewer. Indeed the defensiveness of both men, considering that their careers peaked in what was supposed to have become a meritocratic society, would have interested any psychologist.

Their very names provide material for a social historian. They grew up in an England rich with Normans and Cecils, where young men Brylcreemed their hair and the excitement of the week was going to the pictures on Saturday night. Cecil, the last man in England to use Brylcreem, always remained a film buff, collecting videos and admitting to a particular penchant for Marlon Brando.

Even more than Norman, Cecil was a true case of a working-class graduate to Thatcherism. His father was a Lancashire railwayman; his mother came from an immigrant Catholic family from Belfast. He rose through the meritocratic pre-comprehensive grammar school system. He seems to have been model material for the system – a scholarship boy *par excellence*, talented in the classroom and a valiant performer on the sports field too. When he moved on from the Royal Lancaster Grammar School to Emmanuel College, Cambridge, he ran for the university in the 220 and 440 yards.

Originally he had apparently given the college admission authorities the impression that his ambitions inclined towards the Church. The picture of a Reverend Cecil delivering sermons to the faithful is a fetching one, but in fact before he went up to Cambridge he had decided that this was not for him. He wrote a polite letter informing the Master of Emmanuel of his change of career plans, and received a charming reply pointing out gently that it would have been more appropriate 'to write an *enquiring* letter'. He studied English Literature (under the terrifying Leavis) but then changed his mind again and switched to Law. He went on to qualify as an accountant.

The most important contribution of Cambridge to his education was that it helped him develop as a social animal. By the time he left the university he was the kind of young man who could be taken home to tea in the Home Counties.

So far as university politics were concerned he seems to have been an observer rather than a participant. There was little doubt, however, about his political allegiance in his university days: he was a Labour supporter – yet another Thatcherite who got there via the door on the left. He once went to a Union debate to watch Herbert Morrison and was embarrassed to see that great Labour personality annihilated by Ian Macleod: there were no hints at Cambridge that it would be Parkinson who would, not so very long afterwards, succeed Macleod as Conservative MP for Enfield West.

His grammar school days had been spent under the post-war Labour government and he rationalized later: 'I found Mr Attlee's ideas really attractive. One looks at nationalization now and wonders how anyone can support it. But looking back, after the war it seemed the perfect answer – managers and workers working together for the good of the nation. I'd heard about the 1930s, particularly in the North. It was time for a new course of action, a different sort of society. It gripped my imagination.'

But once away from the university, and working as an accountant in the City, there were other things to grip the imagination, as he continued to sanitize his Northern accent. Cecil soon showed commercial skills in being able to turn round ailing companies, on his own or in conjunction with his father-in-law, after marriage to the daughter of a well-to-do Hertfordshire building contractor. He refined his concept of 'managers and workers working together for the good of the nation'. By his late twenties he was beginning to see the political future in terms of the Opportunity Society. If the railwayman's son from Lancashire could do it, so could others.

When he became active in Hertfordshire Tory politics he was typical of many young men who were beginning to become influential on the lower rungs of the party ladder in the Sixties. At the top, Harold Macmillan might still be talking the patrician language of *noblesse oblige*, that God was in his heaven and all was well with the world. Out there in the suburbs, the party was being run by the Normans and the Cecils who knew that the Lord helps him who helps himself.

Cecil entered Parliament in 1970, in the by-election caused by the death of Ian Macleod. Ted Heath had recently become Prime Minister, on a platform which was supposed to turn the party's back on the old Macmillanite heresies, and Cecil fitted easily into the new breed of Tory MPs who were going to help him do it. His first political job was as a junior Whip under Heath. But when the Heath government began to be accused of slipping into the old heresies itself, his Whip's job did not prevent Cecil from simultaneously getting involved with a coterie of Members, centred around Nicholas Ridley, who used to meet to discuss how far the Cabinet was being blown off course: the party took a very civilized attitude in those days to government supporters with Doubts. When the Heath government fell in confusion in 1974, there was not much doubt about where Cecil's sympathies would lie in the ructions which eventually led to Ted being replaced by Margaret. Cecil, as he himself was to say later, was attracted to strong women. Mrs Parkinson, daughter of a prominent local personality, had been a powerful support to his political and business career. He now gave valuable support to the party's new woman leader.

Ironically, a third woman was already in his life, although few recognized the significance of the fact. Sara Keays had become his secretary shortly after he entered the Commons. The relationship between Cecil and Mrs Thatcher continued during the Falklands War, when the Prime Minister came to rely heavily on his judgement, and during the run-up to the 1983 election campaign which he ran as party chairman. It was at the party conference after that election, which should have been a happy victory celebration, that the *affaire* Parkinson blew up in the faces of the party leadership. Nobody came out of it with much glory. What did it tell us about the ethos of the Thatcher era?

The Profumo episode, in retrospect, was said to have marked the beginning of the end for Harold Macmillan. Certainly Margaret showed more worldly wisdom than Harold did. Whatever else may have survived of her Methodist upbringing, she was not a woman whose automatic instinct, when colleagues confessed to adultery, was to show them the door. She showed Cecil her own kind of loyalty, tempered by a shrewd political assessment of what price the political market would bear.

He had been destined for the Foreign Office in 1983 in the post-election reshuffle. The railwayman's son had come a long way. The Leader liked his sleek good looks, but even more she liked his complete loyalty to the ideals that were hers. She was fed up with a Cabinet that contained doubters. Cecil was completely trustworthy. But when she was informed, privately, of the Keays pregnancy, she deemed that it would be more discreet for him to be promoted to a slightly less high-profile job. That put her in a stronger position, once the storm broke, to be resolute that there was no reason for him to resign. But when the storm refused to go away, she agreed, reluctantly that there was no option.

No one knows whether Cecil was unique among Thatcher ministers in having fathered a child out of wedlock. If the Keays affair had led to remarriage after a discreetly handled divorce – which is what both Cecil and Sarah seem for a time to have assumed – the Conservative party of the 1980s could have handled the situation. Equally, Conservatives in the mid-Eighties were prepared to handle what did happen, a renunciation of Miss Keays, and the saving of the Parkinson marriage, although obviously the party would have been happier if it could have happened with Miss Keays keeping her mouth shut. Either way, Conservatives of the Eighties – the party which puts the family first – could have kept their conscience clear. That was a measure of the change in attitudes over a generation, since the days when divorce could mean political death. What had not changed was a horror of scandal . . . *Pas devant les domestiques*! It was Enoch Powell who once said that humbug is the necessary lubricant of public life.

Everyone agreed that Cecil must do penance before he

could be brought back into the Cabinet. The question was for how long? Willie Whitelaw, who still had a knack of getting his own way, had old-fashioned views about this kind of scandal. His leader, on the other hand, would have settled for the briefest penance. Did she still think, as she looked with distaste at the rest of the ministerial material available, that Cecil was the best bet as a successor?

When he came back, it was not as Foreign Secretary. It was in the humbler role of Energy Secretary – but this, we were assured, was the key job of the moment. He was to handle the denationalization of electricity, which was to be the showpiece of the privatization programme. Indeed, he attracted admiration in the free-market camp as stories circulated about how he was standing up to the vested interests of the industry – he wasn't going to make the mistakes of the earlier denationalizations by ending up with a privatized monopoly. On the Thatcherite wing, the future seemed reasonably secure. Cecil would move on to become Chancellor – a much safer pair of hands than that unpredictable Nigel Lawson, they were saying. After that, who knows, perhaps the Keays affair could be forgotten and he would move – smoothly – from No. 11 into No. 10.

In fact, it didn't work out like that. Electricity privatization did not go as well as they had thought. Cecil was savaged by the select committee which looked at the subject. In the next reshuffle, when he was moved to Transport, all the talk about how he was now to pull off the greatest privatization of them all – British Rail – could not conceal the truth, that Cecil was finally on the way out. It was not Sarah Keays who had done for him, it was his less than sparkling performance as a minister. At Transport, indeed, he looked to be something of a yesterday's man. Except among the dogmatists, the imperative of the 1990s seemed to be the need for a good public service system rather than a wholly privatized one. Things had come full circle.

In November 1990, when the seemingly impossible happened and the great changeover finally came, it seemed only natural, and a little bit sad, when the Transport Minister announced that he would not be seeking a job in the new Major government.

When John Major fought his first election as Prime Minister in 1992, Cecil must have had some ambivalent thoughts – and it showed, when he had to pronounce on the Tories' prospects, as inevitably he was invited to do during the 1992 campaign: Cecil was still a notably photogenic commentator on current affairs, high on the TV producers' lists of performers who were good value for money. Cecil the Thatcherite found it hard to accept that the John Major campaign, fought the way it was fought, could succeed. But the old pro in him as one-time party chairman must have rejoiced when John upset the odds and won. We now await the publication of his biography, as yet untitled. Will it be called *Hell hath no fury* or *Leading Man*?

4

'Tell it like it is'

NICHOLAS RIDLEY

In a composite group portrait of Thatcherites, Nick Ridley stands out easily: he is the one with the cigarette in his mouth. One feels that if Nick had not been a smoker already, he would have taken it up deliberately when non-smoking, like protecting the ozone layer and abolishing apartheid, became part of the stock-in-trade of do-gooders. Nick Ridley was one of those people who can't stand cant. Hermann Goering is supposed to have said that when people began to talk of culture he reached for his revolver. Nick Ridley, confronted with knee-jerk liberals, simply annihilated his opponents with a few terse phrases, sometimes elegant, sometimes downright brutal. He was not a man for wishy-washy liberals to tangle with.

He could, and did, claim to have been a Thatcherite before Thatcher. And to the end he was her staunchest ally on the poll tax and the defence of the pound against a single European currency. His commitment can be traced back to 1965 when he voted for Enoch Powell to become leader of the Conservative party in the election won by Ted Heath (the third candidate, and for a time the favourite to win, being

Reggie Maudling). When the Shadow Cabinet, under Ted, met at the Selsdon Park Hotel to pin their colours to the mast of market economics, Nick became Selsdon Man incarnate. When Ted became Prime Minister a few months later, he made him a junior minister at the Department of Trade and Industry, a key department in the grand privatization programme that would have been the logical sequel to Selsdon.

It didn't work out that way. Nick was soon disillusioned by the Heath U-turn. Offered sideways promotion (to become Minister for the Arts), he decided that Ted-style government was not for him. He thus joined the fairly small band of politicians who have resigned on a point of principle. Ted claims he was sacked. Accomplished amateur painter that he was, Nick would have made an interesting Arts Minister. So, for that matter, would Ted, the accomplished amateur musician. But in 1972 both saw their destinies as lying elsewhere.

Nick returned to the back benches, where he proceeded to prove how effective back-bench politics can be. He was one of a group of clever Members – others were John Biffen and Jock Bruce-Gardyne – who became a sort of resistance movement against the Conservative government. What we were seeing, in fact, although few people realized it at the time, was the start of a division of the party between what came to be called the wets and the dries. The dries had got hold of what was then the little-known, arcane science of monetarism. As Ted wrestled with prices and incomes policies and all the other dramas of the mid-Seventies, the activities of Nick, John and Jock were watched with interest from inside the Cabinet by its token woman, the Education Secretary Margaret Thatcher. She sympathized, and told them she sympathized. But she remained in the government. It was her kind of loyalty.

Of course, it is all too easy to oversimplify the division that was taking place in the Conservative party. As was to be pointed out *ad nauseam* over the next twenty years, Nick Ridley superficially possessed all the qualities that came to be regarded as belonging to the paid-up wet. He had been educated at Eton and (worse) Balliol. Government was in his blood: he was the tenth Ridley to sit in the House of Commons. Again, in contrast to many of the most earnest monetarists in the research institutes and the pressure groups of the Seventies and Eighties, he had actually worked in industry and knew about practical things like balance sheets and dealing with trade unions. He has described how he took a dislike to nationalization during his Oxford days, which was when the Attlee government was nationalizing everything. 'Later,' he wrote, 'when I was working with Brims & Co., building shipyards on the banks of the Tyne, I found practical experience confirmed my objections. There was a sloppiness about the way public corporations behaved.'

In his spare time he was a country gentleman, skilled at casting for salmon, or, in more mellow mood, painting his pleasant water-colours. He had been brought up in rural Northumberland. 'I had to spend half of each school holiday working with the farm workers, or the woodmen, the masons, the joiners or the gardeners, learning their trade.' He has put on record, in crisp words, that he did not see why, when he became Secretary of State for the Environment, he should be lectured by town dwellers about conservation. He was a countryman: 'What is a countryman? Someone brought up in the countryside, experiencing the cycle of the seasons. He has seen a stoat kill a rabbit and a sparrow-hawk kill a song-thrush. He knows how to catch the trout in the brook and flight a wild duck in the evening. He knows the wild flowers and the butterflies . . .'

And there was more than that to Nick. He had the background too of an artistic heritage. His maternal grandfather was the architect Lutyens. But above all, the observers of Tory wetness and dryness noted, he was an aristo, the younger son of a viscount. Such people, in the Seventies and Eighties, tended to treat the Thatcherites as regrettable *arrivistes*. In Nick's case his background simply made him a

Thatcherite with style, who didn't give a damn whether people liked his style or not. He was the only Gentleman Monetarist.

His personal loyalty to his leader was never in doubt. The earthy part of his nature made him well aware of failings in Margaret Thatcher's character that some of those close to her never seemed to see. But to the whole persona he showed a devotion that was striking in one who could be so cynical. He identified completely with the power structure as it developed in Downing Street during the 1980s. He had no reservations about Margaret Thatcher's interpretation of the role of Prime Minister. That interpretation has never been so clearly articulated from within her own camp, sometimes with unconsciously devastating frankness, as by Nicholas Ridley in the book he wrote after they had both left office: *My Style of Government, The Thatcher Years.*

In the book he quotes with approval a voice from the first Elizabethan age: Francis Bacon, who pointed out in his essay 'On Counsel' the importance of the seating arrangements when decisions are taken: 'A long table, and a square table, or seats about the walls, seem things of form, but are things of substance; for at the long table a few at the upper end in effect sway all the business; but in the other forms there is more use of the counsellors' opinions that sit lower.' Margaret Thatcher, Nicholas Ridley noted, definitely preferred a long table. He added: 'She was Prime Minister, she knew what she wanted to do, and she didn't believe her policies should be subject to being voted down by a group she had selected to advise and assist her.'

Much of the Ridley argument was based on what many would consider a questionable comparison with the position of a President of the United States, where 'the Executive consists of one person with supreme power and supreme responsibility'. Given a Presidential style of government, all else followed so far as Nick was concerned: the determination not to be dictated to by officials in Brussels; the fact that she had no time for the 'feeling in the Tory party that each strand of opinion in the party should be represented at Cabinet'. For political colleagues and for senior civil servants 'the test was "Are you here to help or to hinder" – it seems to me a reasonable question for the Head of Government to ask.' The Cabinet was 'very much a formal body', not a decision-making instrument, except for decisions of the very greatest importance. It was also a court of appeal, although seldom used as such, to which an individual minister could bring a disagreement with a colleague.

Clearly it was a system where much depended on the wisdom of appointments made by 'the person with supreme power'. Ridley in his book admitted that Margaret did not always choose well, but he had some fascinating comments to make on the people she liked to work with. Lord King 'was the sort of man she admired, a tough and determined customer'. As to Bernard Ingham, Nick indicates that he thoroughly approved of his decision as press secretary to provide the Prime Minister with only a summary sheet of what the newspapers were saying each day, thus protecting her from the full impact of attacks from 'the intelligentsia' of the press.

Nick's own career as a Thatcher minister began as Minister of State at the Foreign and Commonwealth Office. Some claimed later to detect in this appointment one of the rare recorded examples of Margaret playing a practical joke – putting Nick in a position where he had to use diplomacy. Their relationship was something like that of a stern schoolmistress happy to indulge a brilliant but wayward pupil. There is a story from the days shortly after she had become party leader about how Nick invited the monetarist Economic Dining Club, of which she was a member, to meet in his flat where he was to cook the dinner. He was at that time between marriages, and the dining club were greatly interested when they were interrupted by a lady friend of Nick's who had mistaken the evening when *she* was due to come for dinner. Margaret, he recalls, 'teased me mercilessly.'

At the Foreign Office Nick nearly pulled off a diplomatic

51

coup. He had oversight of what in 1979 was regarded as the boring problem of the long-standing dispute with Argentina over ownership of the Falkland Islands. He persuaded the Galtieri regime in Buenos Aires to consider a formula whereby sovereignty would pass to Argentina but the islands would be leased back, to maintain an effective status quo for the islanders. Such a formula, practical and cost-effective, he presumably saw as being well within the rules of market economics as he understood them. Back home, the Conservative party didn't see it that way at all, and neither did the Prime Minister, who was just recovering from the painful experience of agreeing, against her instincts, to resolve the Rhodesia question by granting independence to Zimbabwe. There was much huffing and puffing over the Ridley solution. Then the Falklands were forgotten for the time being – except in Argentina.

Nick was soon forgiven, as was proved when he was moved from the FCO to the boiler-room of the Thatcherite government. He became Financial Secretary to the Treasury – a position held in Victorian times, he was pleased to recall, by his great-grandfather. At last, at the Treasury, he was able to take part in the process of selling off the nationalized industries. He also came face to face with the extent of Britain's financial contribution to the EEC and how it was calculated. It did not endear him to the 'European ideal'. In fact, the Treasury job confirmed him as 'One of Us'.

He was ready for Cabinet, which he entered as Transport Secretary and where he continued his career as a privatizer. He sold off the National Bus Company, dividing it into seventy-two different companies. He prepared British Airways and the British Airports Authority for sale. Meanwhile he contributed to the Thatcherite vision of free trading links with Europe by giving the go-ahead for the Channel Tunnel. Next came the Department of the Environment, where privatization meant selling off the water boards. It was at Environment that the public really got to know Nick. In his thankless role as arbiter on planning permissions, Nick the countryman came face to face with the NIMBY syndrome – everybody is keen in theory to see new housing built, or other useful developments, but Not in My Back Yard. Embarrassment came when he objected to a planning application near his own country home. It was all a typical piece of media mischief, he observed irritably.

Environment is a high-profile job. One day he found himself in a car with the Prime Minister between Heathrow and London. Being driven along the highway is one of the few opportunities that modern Prime Ministers have to see part of the world that the rest of us live in. The road from Heathrow was filthy with litter. The Secretary of State for the Environment found himself getting an ear-battering from the Prime Minister for not keeping Britain tidier. The rest is history. Some time later the media were invited to send their cameras to a prearranged spot in St James's Park to watch the Prime Minister, with her faithful Environment Secretary at her side, picking up rubbish, at least some of it laid out with care earlier that morning by DoE staff.

But this was the mere cosmetics of the job. Environment also meant the Community Charge. Nick didn't invent the Community Charge. It had been agreed in principle before he arrived at Environment. Margaret was determined to abolish the rates, which she saw as a penalty on property-owners who improve their property. Nick for his part was very conscious that the system of rates rebates had come to mean that there were areas where the majority of the population paid nothing to the local authorities they elected. He accepted that the Community Charge was the most practical way to replace the rates, assuming that the level of the charge was reasonable. He had not reckoned on the size of local authority budgets. There was sometimes a sort of unworldliness in Nick's makeup. Nor, although he was happy to cope with Labour critics, was he prepared for the criticisms that built up among Tory back-benchers as the complexities of the poll tax began to emerge.

Perhaps the poll tax was a no-win situation from the start, however sound the principle. Before it ever raised a penny, many Conservatives were beginning to feel in their bones that they were watching the birth of a potential election-loser. Could Nicholas Ridley have prevented that? Given the Prime Minister's determination, no Environment Secretary could have stopped the poll tax getting on to the statute book. But many Tories had suspicions that the combination of the Prime Minister and this particular Environment Secretary was not calculated to show a sure touch in coping with the anxieties of the electorate. Nick himself was not sorry to leave the DoE when, in 1989, he became Secretary of State for Trade and Industry. The Thatcher government was now, although few of us suspected it, entering its final phase, a phase dominated by the issue of the EEC.

At one time Nick Ridley had been an enthusiast for 'Europe'. In the Sixties he had been a delegate to the Council of Europe and at that time was once even accused by a jocular colleague in the House of being a 'federast'. As a minister he was disillusioned about the federal ambitions of the Brussels establishment. By the late Eighties he took the same min-imalist approach as the Prime Minister: *their* European ideal was simply a free trade area. They did not want West-minster to lose control over Britain's currency. They wanted no truck with the Delors Plan. They saw events in the Soviet Union and eastern Europe as being a good reason for slowing, not accelerating, progress towards European unity.

Until the late 1980s it was possible for Thatcherite econ-omics to be a broad enough church to contain a variety of interpretations of the European ideal. As the time came for hard decisions to be made, a polarization was inevitable among ministers whose Thatcherite credentials up until then were thought to have been impeccable. In his resignation speech, Nigel Lawson described how as Chancellor in late 1988 he had proposed to the Prime Minister 'a fully worked-out scheme for the independence of the Bank of England' – making it more like the German Bundesbank and less under the control, so to speak, of Mrs Thatcher.

Mrs Thatcher said No. She had set out her own approach in the famous Bruges speech of September 1988. She had now a tight-knit group of allies to stand up against Delors, not least the formidable No. 10 secretary Charles Powell. Nick Ridley was an enthusiastic supporter and was convinced that her authority, once threatened by Cabinet wets who had long since departed, was now being conspired against by no less than her Chancellor and her Deputy Prime Minister, Geoffrey Howe. He also knew, as the Prime Minister did, that there was a lot of gut sympathy out there among ordinary voters for 'standing up to foreigners'. Ordinary people didn't like the French. They still treated the Germans as the enemy. Anti-EEC activists often waged their campaign at two levels. There was an intellectual argument, conducted publicly, about economic dangers. Underneath was the unspoken argument which was that we wanted no truck with untrustworthy foreigners.

It was wholly typical of Nick that he got into trouble by speaking the unspeakable. In fairness, he seems not to have done so deliberately for publication. He made his remark during what he thought was an off-the-record part of an interview with the *Spectator*. He soon knew better. There were the damning words in print, along with a cartoon indicating that he thought of Herr Kohl as being like Hitler.

Nick, the languid aristo, always seemed to have difficulty in determining when it was acceptable to put thoughts into words. He seemed to be genuinely taken aback when Geoffrey Howe, in *his* resignation speech, revealed how he had been seething with indignation at his treatment by the Prime Minister but had never voiced it till now. Nick seemed to want one rule for himself and another

for others. In any event, after the *Spectator* article he had
to go. Margaret lost yet another stalwart member of the praetorian guard. It was only a matter of time before she went
too.

5

The other woman
EDWINA CURRIE

THE RELATIONSHIP between Thatcherism and the women's liberation movement is beyond the scope of this book. Britain's first woman Prime Minister was, notoriously, slow to pack her Cabinet with women. But at one point during the late 1980s there was an opinion poll which showed that the best-known member of the government, apart from herself, was a woman.

There were similarities between Edwina Currie and Margaret Thatcher, similarities which Edwina, never guilty of hiding her light under a bushel, was not slow to mention. For a start, the two women shared the same birthday. They both came from families fairly far down the social pecking order, the sort of families not well represented in the decision-making strata of the Conservative party. In Edwina's case the background was Liverpool Jewish. 'You can take the girl out of Liverpool,' it was said of her, 'but you can't take Liverpool out of the girl.'

Both women were examples of what is meant by a merito-cratic society. Like Margaret Thatcher, Edwina got her foot firmly on the career ladder by winning a place at Oxford to read chemistry. Both found it easy to survive and prosper in essentially male worlds. At university, Edwina remembered, 'most of my time was spent at the Oxford Union, then as now dominated by chaps'.

Both women had backgrounds which in the past would have tended to send an ambitious young person into the Labour party, but neither Margaret nor Edwina ever seems to have been remotely tempted by the politics of the Left. Edwina first hit the headlines indeed as the darling of the floggers and hangers of our great party when she used a pair of handcuffs as a visual aid at the Conservative conference of 1981. If both of them were natural right-wingers, however, they certainly did not fit into the old right wing of the party. Both, frankly, had a grating effect on the people who used to run the Tory party. Neither could have cared less.

In some ways it is Edwina rather than Margaret whose character tells us what was happening to the Conservative party during the last quarter of the twentieth century. Never judge a party just by the people at Westminster. At the grass roots, it is the women who give our party its backbone, and you could tell a lot about us by looking around the body of the hall at the annual conference. At one time the uniform of the archetypal conference representative was twin-set and pearls and sensible shoes. Things changed. Colour schemes became vibrant. Highlights appeared in hair styles. Heels got higher. Shoulder pads made their presence felt. In the old days you had the feeling that the husbands left behind were happy to get back to their grouse moors. Now, one felt, the husbands were busy running their car dealerships on the Kingston bypass.

It was a social revolution. It would be wrong to say that Edwina merged naturally into the new background because Edwina never merged into anything in her life. But it seemed her natural habitat. She carried with her, somebody once said, the ambience of Benidorm-on-Thames.

She rose up the Tory hierarchy by the local government

route. She was the youngest member of the Birmingham City Council, and before long was chairman of its Social Services Committee, responsible, as she liked to recall later, for a budget of over £50 million and a staff of 8,000. This was a woman who, once elected as an MP, assumed that her natural role was running a Whitehall department.

A bright young man in her position would have been given sage counsel by the old hands at Westminster – who are the right people to butter up, when is the right time to keep one's head down, that sort of thing. He would have been warned of the dangers of pushiness. He would have been warned of the dangers of being too open with the media. By contrast, Edwina could be said to have raised pushiness to an art form. Journalists found themselves being telephoned and told they would hear something to their advantage if they invited her to lunch.

The chemistry between Edwina and the media worked quickly. Reporters appreciate politicians who can provide instant quotes on practically everything. Press photographers like woman politicians of striking appearance who are willing to brandish things in front of a camera. The handcuffs technique was developed and refined. The stuffier elements in the party were distressed, but news editors and picture editors were grateful.

Edwina's political preferment came with her appointment as parliamentary private secretary to the scholarly Sir Keith Joseph when he was Education Secretary. It seems an unlikely partnership until you remember that nobody has ever questioned the sharpness of the Currie brain – when she became a minister herself, civil servants were impressed, and sometimes alarmed, by her extraordinary speed in mastering briefs.

Cleverness, though, has never earned many brownie points in the Conservative party. Cleverness *and* pushiness – and in a female – are seen as downright subversive. The traditionalists, of whom there were still a fair number on the

Conservative back benches even in the Eighties, were notably underwhelmed by Edwina, but they accepted the logic of events when she was promoted to be a junior minister in a reshuffle of the Thatcher government in 1986. She was talented, she was young, she was ambitious. And her Thatcherite credentials appeared to be impeccable.

If it was hoped that office would shut her up, it was simply not in the nature of the creature. Edwina launched into her ministerial career with all the solemnity of a motor racing champion squirting a magnum of champagne in the faces of his friends after winning the grand prix. Sensitive souls at Westminster still wince at the memory of the day Edwina became a minister. The reshuffle, and her possible part in it, had been the subject of much media discussion beforehand. In the public interest, Edwina agreed that on the day when the Prime Minister would be putting her list together, a television crew should be sited in the Currie garden with a camera trained through the window at the telephone which, it was assumed, would surely ring to summon her to Downing Street. The phone duly rang, the camera duly rolled. Millions of viewers were privileged to take part in a moment of televisual history. From then on, the cameras never seemed to stop rolling.

Her job was at the Department of Health. In a non-interventionist government, this was one of the few departments where, in the late Eighties, it was deemed proper for the government to tell people how to run their lives. The man in Whitehall knew best. So did the woman. It was official policy that we should stop smoking, cut down on fatty foods, refrain from catching AIDS and (if elderly) try to get through the winter without dying of hypothermia. The scope for a vociferous, self-confident, media-conscious minister was almost limitless. Edwina was photographed performing on exercise bicycles, having her cholesterol tested, and advising the old to 'buy long-johns, check your hot-water bottles, knot gloves and scarves and get your grandchildren to give you a woolly night-cap'. On matters sexual she entered into detail that would once have incurred a charge of corrupting the morals of the young.

For years, it had been part of all ministers' jobs to expose themselves to photo-opportunities. They put on hard hats and strode across windswept building sites; they embraced visitors from important but remote places abroad; they quaffed strange beverages; they squeezed their posteriors into minuscule chairs in infant classrooms; they peered into the entrails of machinery they did not understand – all the time making appropriate noises and passing on the approved messages.

Edwina took all this forward by a quantum leap. She grasped, as few ministers had done before, that there is all the difference in the world between providing worthy quotes for the media which end up, if you are lucky, as an inch of small type at the bottom of page 8 of the *Independent*, and dreaming up something shocking that makes a headline on the front page of the *Sun*. If society needed to be shocked into avoiding AIDS or cervical cancer, then Edwina was the person to do it.

The shock tactics were applied not just to health propaganda but also to the politics of market economics. Why did we not, she demanded, 'postpone that second holiday and use the money for a non-urgent operation?' Why did we not 'put off decorating the living-room and get our teeth done instead?' Again, about half of Britain's pensioners were house-owners: why shouldn't they sell the equity of their homes and pay for their health care privately?

Part of the reason the Conservative party was always uneasy with Edwina was that her propaganda covered such a broad canvas. She came out with bone-dry messages that delighted the Thatcherite ultras – until they remembered that this same woman seemed dangerously close to the liberal establishment on matters to do with health (particularly women's health) and the protection of the environment. Meanwhile, on the non-Thatcherite, or pre-Thatcherite, wing of the party the knights of the shires wondered sadly if this was what they had come into politics for, and wished Edwina would go away. In the late Eighties, of course, nobody bothered much about what knights of the shires said or thought. Then, unpredictably, their moment arrived. The drama of eggs, Edwina and the knights of the shires is an object lesson in how the most unlikely events can turn politics on its head.

The health risks in British-produced eggs had been an issue for months. But it was one of those boring issues that interest only experts and cranks, a matter of statistical tables and scientific jargon, and with overtones (because most of the eggs were produced in factory farming conditions) of animal liberation and suchlike. Evidence of salmonella in eggs was passed around the Whitehall departments and the farming organizations without much being done about it. This was the kind of situation that Edwina saw as crying out for her talents. One Saturday night on the TV news she was seen announcing that 'most of the country's egg production' was affected by salmonella.

As it happened, this was not factually accurate. She should have said 'much of' rather than 'most of' – but then, under-statement was not part of her stock in trade. It was not statisti-cal niceties that really caused the trouble. The combination of eggs, Currie and television was explosive. As a publicist, Edwina had reached a critical mass, so to speak, at that point in her ministerial career. Like a pop singer who can pick up even an indifferent song and take it to the top of the charts, Edwina had found a formula for making ordinary people believe that if she was worried about something, they ought to be worrying too. Egg sales dropped overnight by 15 per cent. Eggs became a major political issue. The Prime Minister found herself telling the world, with the same seriousness that she might have used to warn of the dangers of a single European currency, that she had just had scrambled eggs for lunch 'and enjoyed it'.

The Conservative party at the end of the 1980s had changed mightily since it was run in the way that seemed right to the knights of the shires as they looked out at the world from their broad acres. And farming had changed out of all recognition since the days when a farmyard was a place where the rosy-cheeked farmer's wife went out to cast corn at the chickens clucking happily on the dung-heap. But one thing had not changed: when the chips were down, the Conservative party knew it could not afford to cross the farming lobby. The farming lobby – the knights of the shires, the factory farmers, the new breed of accountant-farmers – they all knew where their duty lay. Currie must go. Currie went, unlamented by her boss, Kenneth Clarke.

There was a wisp of a smile on some knightly faces. It was, as another woman politician was shortly to observe, a funny old world.

After what would have appeared as a decent period of silence, Edwina surfaced during the March 1992 election campaign. She complained – at a time when the party's campaign tactics were coming under fire – that John Major standing on a soap box made a Daimler-driven Neil Kinnock look like the Prime Minister, and John Major, the Leader of the Opposition. After the Conservative party's surprising victory, Edwina was quoted as saying 'I got it wrong.'

This 'sally' was greeted by the nodding of grey heads. A day or so later she announced to the nation that she had refused the Prime Minister's kind offer of promotion to the rank of Minister of State at the Home Office, in charge of prisons. Was the offer not a good one? Edwina seemed to think not, although there was much speculation as to her reasons. Could it have been that the new Home Secretary was Kenneth Clarke, under whom she had hatched her eggs at the Department of Health? Could it have been the relative poverty of high office? Edwina must be earning from her media activities something in the range of £200,000 a year. Could it have been that she wanted to be returned as a

Euro-MP, looking, as it were, for new fields to conquer? Whatever the reasons, Edwina still sits upon the back benches: the woman who had once boasted in the House of providing her husband with, among other things, 'a steamy bed', seems, for the time being at least, to have come to the end of the road.

6

The lad who wanted to be a policeman
NEIL KINNOCK

THE PRE-THATCHER age came to an end with a whimper one spring evening in 1979 when the minority Labour government was no longer able to muster any majority at all in the division lobbies. Premier Callaghan made a dignified little announcement that he would submit to the will of the electorate, and departed. It was left to a largely unknown young Welsh Member called Kinnock to assemble a group of back-benchers in the gangway of the Chamber and lead the singing of 'The Red Flag'. Ten years later the Labour party was more into *Tannhäuser* and Beethoven's Ninth for musical inspiration, with TV pictures of that nice couple, Neil and Glenys, walking slowly into the sunset, but in the 1970s Labour consisted largely of unreconstructed socialists. That was one reason why Margaret Thatcher was able to trounce Labour at the polls in May 1979. And during at least the earlier years of the Thatcher regime the Opposition was still a party that had not moved too far from Keir Hardie and Clause 4.

Mrs Thatcher was a lucky Prime Minister. Part of her luck lay in the Labour leaders she had to face. After Jim Callaghan came Michael Foot, that distinguished old man of letters who gave the impression of being no more at home in 1980s politics than Soames Forsyte would have been had he been dropped into a City office full of yuppies and electronic screens. And after Michael came Neil.

Neil's pedigree as a potential party leader was as impeccable as that of the 14th Earl of Home when he, twenty years before, was picked to lead the Tories. Neil's father and grandfather were both miners, automatic members of the Labour aristocracy. The Welsh working-class ethos was in his mother's milk. It was a tough, lusty ethos – not always in tune with the modern left-wingers who dine on a nut roast washed down with a lively Cabernet Sauvignon from Romania and talk about sexism in the *Sun*. Neil was not a nut-roast person. In some quarters it was often noted, more in anger than in sorrow, that he was 'a man's man'.

His enjoyment of Rugby football, and of singing the kind of songs they sing at Cardiff Arms Park, was no affectation. There was a distinctly rough side to Neil. People who insulted him or his family were liable to be threatened with fisticuffs. A likeable trait in some, but it scarcely added up to a personality calculated to have Margaret Thatcher trembling in her shoes.

His limitations became clear, for instance, during the miners' strike. There were powerful arguments he might have used to increase public understanding of the issues at stake in those troubled times. Instead, when he faced Mrs Thatcher across the despatch box, the rhetoric was born of gut feelings that came straight from the Valleys. There was a suggestion of the special kind of emotion, not calculated to appeal to the Prime Minister of 1984, with which Harold Macmillan used to talk, misty-eyed, about the British miner as the salt of the earth.

Harold Macmillan, when he chose to talk about miners, was wont to go on to talk about the horrors of the mud of Flanders. Interestingly, Neil, several generations too late for Flanders, seems to have shared the idea of the British miner and the British Tommy as archetypal noble figures. At school in South

Wales, where he was not an outstanding scholar, he apparently begged his parents to be allowed to leave to join the Army – or the police. One can picture his lean figure, with close-cropped ginger hair, fitting into the barrack-room. One can see him exchanging carefully worded banter with the sergeant-major and downing pints of an evening with the boys down at the Naafi. But it was not to be. The young Kinnock was persuaded to get back to his books and was packed off to University College, Cardiff (where he met Glenys). In due course the Welsh Constabulary's loss was to be the Labour party's gain.

His student days were the heady Sixties. They were the days of 'We will overcome' and conviction politics. The world was to be transformed by the charisma of John F. Kennedy. Neil and Glenys seem to have been a familiar couple on the campus, leading the singing of protest songs. It was a time when political commitment was a matter of lofty ideals rather than detailed analysis of economic policy. They belonged – and he acknowledged that he belonged – to the 'never had it so good' era. Later, making the point that he was the first of the Kinnocks to have got to university, he was to say that his generation had been born, relatively speaking, with golden spoons in their mouths. Like many an actor on the Thatcherite stage, he had learned his lines in the Swinging Sixties.

He became a tutor-organizer with the Workers' Educational Association. It was a job that some socialists might have used as a base for meaningful research: 'Patterns of Discrimination in the Post-Industrial Society', 'Workers' Rights in the Social Market Context' – that sort of thing. But Neil was not the academic kind of tutor. The job helped him to develop as a speaker. 'The Welsh windbag', they called him when he reached Westminster, but the fact was that Neil on a good day was a very good speaker indeed. The WEA job also brought good contacts in industrial South Wales. He impressed the local Labour establishment. At the age of 28 he became Labour MP for Bedwellty.

He arrived in the House at the time when Ted Heath had just ousted Harold Wilson as Prime Minister. Neil fell naturally among those members of the parliamentary party who took it for granted that the reason Labour was out in the cold yet again was that Wilson had not been socialist enough. His instincts were to taunt the 'right wing' of the party. (Later, when Roy Jenkins stood for the Labour leadership, Neil liked to repeat the story that went the rounds at Westminster about an old miner MP being asked whether he would vote for Roy. 'Nay, lad,' was the reply, 'we're all Labour here.') As a young MP he was not over-kind to the Labour front bench: 'They treat the City of London as if it were some kind of winnable Tory marginal constituency.' He gravitated naturally into the Tribune Group.

A turning point in his career came at the 1975 Labour conference. An important part of the annual Tribune rally held at conference time is the taking of the collection. In 1975, Neil, still a stripling in his early 30s, was given the honour of making the 'collection speech', the original speaker having been dropped because of some last-minute twist in the Byzantine politics of the Tribunites. He brought the house down – and there was a record collection. 'He's a find, that boy,' wrote Barbara Castle in her diary.

On the Right of the party there was less enthusiasm about the boy. One reason why some right-wingers eventually pulled out of the Labour party to form the Social Democrats was that they saw the new generation of left-wingers, like Neil, coming forward. The Michael Foots of this world could be forgiven – that was the way old men felt. But to see young men who seemed to have forgotten nothing and learned nothing . . .

Nevertheless, Neil was undeniably a bright boy. When Jim Callaghan became Prime Minister he made several attempts to woo Neil into the government. Neil preferred to keep his options open on the back benches. He was never really at home with the Callaghan type of leadership. At the 1977 conference he gave another show-stopping performance, in the 'End of the Peers' revue, where he sang 'Old Man Callaghan' – 'He must know somethin', but he don't do nothing' . . . Neil belonged to the cheeky anti-establishment wing of the party.

When Mrs Thatcher came to power, the Labour party seemed determined to will her to stay there indefinitely. Michael Foot, when elected to succeed Jim, made speeches which could be a joy to listen to but were seldom of more than minimal relevance to the issues of the Thatcher years. He allowed much of the Labour initiative to fall into the hands of the Tony Benns and the Militant activists at Westminster and, out in the country, to people like Derek Hatton in Liverpool and the women at Greenham Common. When Mrs Thatcher faced her second election in 1983, she was up against one of the most ineffective oppositions ever. Labour fought that election on the famously flabby manifesto that was dubbed by Gerald Kaufman 'the longest suicide note in history'.

Neil was deemed to have had a good election in 1983. It gave scope for his talent in full-blooded oratory in the Welsh pulpit tradition: 'If Margaret Thatcher wins on Thursday,' he thundered, 'I warn you not to be ordinary. I warn you not to be young. I warn you not to fall ill. I warn you not to get old.'

The 1983 election did not have to be a Labour débâcle. Mrs Thatcher's biographer, Hugo Young, noted, indeed: 'The most widespread fear gripping senior ministers between autumn 1982 and spring 1983 was that the Labour party would summon itself to dispose of Michael Foot and replace him with Denis Healey . . . Tories feared that Labour would shoot their fox, the aged and uncharismatic Foot, and expose their leader to more equal competition.' Labour didn't, and were humiliated. Afterwards, they recognized that Foot had to go but were divided on whether to opt for another leader of the Left or to go for someone on the Right, Roy Hattersley being seen as fitting the bill. A few clever people, notably Clive Jenkins, thought the solution was to 'skip a generation' and go for Neil. Finally, immensely proud of their own cunning, they came up with the 'dream ticket' – Kinnock as leader and Roy as deputy.

Neil's backers had been more clever than perhaps they realized. The boy from South Wales was growing up. Watching the Thatcher government from the opposition benches, he had become increasingly impatient with the spoilers on the Left of his party. Installed as leader, he set his sights on the Militants of Liverpool – earning the accolade of being described by one Liverpool Labour MP as 'the biggest traitor since Ramsay MacDonald'. In a political roughhouse, Neil was a hard man to beat.

After the ambivalent Michael Foot, the party had found itself a man who could sense a Loony Lefty at thirty paces. More remarkably, he was sometimes even prepared to do something about it. Michael Leapman in his monograph, *Kinnock* – a not unsympathetic work – has written that the first years of the Kinnock leadership 'revealed a streak of ruthlessness previously hidden, a willingness to alienate many who had, in the 1970s, counted themselves his allies'.

In standing up to Mrs Thatcher, ruthlessness may have been a necessary condition: it was not a sufficient one. By the time Neil took over as Leader of the Opposition she and her ministers had had ample time to dig in. They had seen off Michael Foot. Moreover, when Neil came along they were even in a position, as they had not been a year or two earlier, to point to an upturn in the economy. Effective opposition in the House called, therefore, for a degree of subtlety – and certainly for careful research to get the facts right. That was scarcely Neil's way. He was happier when simply getting to his feet, working himself into a peak of righteous indignation, and belting it out.

In the twice-weekly formal confrontations at Prime Minister's Questions he eventually improved, but he never really learned the basic trick at Question Time – that the most potent weapon is brevity. Ministers have been pole-axed by a questioner who knows when to say no more than 'Why?' Alas, that involves more verbal self-discipline than can be expected of the average Member. Questions become double-barrelled, and triple-barrelled . . . 'And finally, Mr Speaker, would the Prime Minister not agree . . .' Oratorical self-indulgence gives easy points to the government. The more bits that are packed into a single question, the easier it is for a minister to ignore all the bits that don't suit him; and the longer the question, the more time he has to think up a devastating response. All this Neil must have known, in theory. But the mellifluous Welsh tones would drone on and on. The style that warmed hearts at a Tribune rally or in a miners' hall had limited appeal to the unconverted. Broad-brush oratory in the tradition of the Valleys was not enough when what was needed was mastery of detail, however – it is often the nitty-gritty, not the grand oratorical gesture, that carries the day in the Commons. Neil failed to wring the advantages out of that ready-made opportunity for a Leader of the Opposition, the Westland affair. He waffled. It was the painstaking John Smith – a lawyer trained to work to a brief – who exposed the government's nerve endings when that tortuous story came to be dissected by the House. The parliamentary Labour party remembered the Smith perform-ance when the time came to replace Neil.

Yet there was an undeniable likeability about Neil that could cross party borders. His irritation with the zealots of the Far Left must have done more for Labour credibility than a year of lectures from Tony Benn. He must have won over floating votes simply by the fact that he wore a suit and a tie and that his hair was short-back-and-sides – not because the image-makers told him to do it but because it came naturally to a well-brought-up boy from the Valleys.

Asked by a feminist magazine, *Everywoman*, for his views on bringing up children, he responded in tones that would have won a few approving nods in commuter trains out of Waterloo to stockbroker Surrey: 'I'm a father. And no matter how much I try to convince myself towards the course of "enlightenment", I know damn well that, put to the test, I'm what people would call a reactionary.' The Labour party had come a long way since Harold Wilson's Swinging Sixties.

By the time of the 1992 general election, the transformation of Kinnock, and the transformation of the Labour party, were complete. The election was to be their moment of triumph. A great deal was written about how much more of a prime ministerial figure he was than John Major. Indeed, the commentators gave hostage after hostage to fortune as the campaign progressed and it seemed that at last Labour had found itself a leader who was a winner. Labour was now a party of government, they said. The Kinnock strategy of muzzling the Left and the loonies had worked. The skilled working classes who had deserted Labour to vote for Mrs Thatcher had been won back. And so on. On polling day the commentators had their noses rubbed in it.

The story of Neil Kinnock is perhaps above all a story simply about the unelectability of the Labour party.

7

Whatever happened to Red Ken?

KEN LIVINGSTONE

BY THE 1990s, Ken Livingstone was no more than one of a group of left-wing Labour MPs whose name cropped up from time to time on the inside pages of newspapers. In the heyday of Thatcherism he was front-page news – the outstanding guerilla leader in the anti-Thatcher resistance movement. Dashing and stylish, like all the best brigands, he knew how to organize lethal sallies down from the mountains and be back there before the forces of authority knew what had hit them. The secret of guerilla warfare is to use minimal force to tie down disproportionately large numbers of government troops. At one time or another, Livingstone had the Cabinet, the Tory back benches, the House of Lords, the judiciary and the high priests of local government livid with impotent anger. Meanwhile the sheer cheek of his operations won cheers even from those who didn't believe in the causes he was fighting for – maybe because, in the grey days of the early 1980s, he could raise a smile when there was little else on the political landscape to laugh about. Livingstone must rank as one of the cheekiest politicians ever.

Should he have been taken seriously? Consider the list of

battles he got involved in. He wondered publicly why we needed a Royal Family. He fought for Gay Rights. He spoke sympathetically of the IRA. There is often a bit of the clown in resistance leaders. They can be such engaging chaps that ordinary citizens forget that out there in the *maquis* some of their friends are pretty nasty people. Ken Livingstone was the smiling, jolly face of fairly extreme socialism. It is a sad commentary on British politics that at the time his kind of socialism seemed to be the most effective opposition to the Thatcher government. Fortunately, at the end of the day, there was little to show for it.

Yet for almost a decade he could not be ignored. He has been described as the only genuinely left-wing leader ever to have achieved real power in England. That he had popular appeal has never been in doubt, even if it was the dubious appeal enjoyed by pop stars or footballers. At the end of 1982 (the year of the Falklands War) in a BBC poll in which Mrs Thatcher was voted Woman of the Year, he came second in the Man of the Year poll – beaten only by the Pope. Then it all slipped away quite quickly. But he is worth remembering if only for one thing. He was one of the few politicians in British history who have created a national presence using local politics. The Chamberlain family did it – Churchill contemptuously called Neville Chamberlain the best Lord Mayor produced by Birmingham in a bad year – but they were exceptional.

Livingstone's centre of operations was the Greater London Council, now no longer in existence, and even then a body which on paper had very little power indeed. Executive power in London local government rested with individual borough councils – the GLC filled a rather shadowy co-ordinating role that scarcely justified its headquarters in the impressive County Hall sited across the Thames from the Houses of Parliament. But on this unlikely foundation, Livingstone built a power base that briefly had massive influence on national politics. He did it by pretending that the GLC was a sort of alternative government that could make good the damage being inflicted by that woman in power across the river.

It followed that the GLC, as well as having a local government policy, had to have a foreign policy (unify Ireland), a defence policy (abolish nuclear weapons within the GLC area), a transport policy (abolish fares) and a comprehensive social policy (largely about affirmative discrimination in favour of women, blacks and homosexuals). As an exercise in local nationalism there had been nothing like it since that masterpiece from Ealing Studios, *Passport to Pimlico*, in which the plot depended on a long-forgotten historical accident that had left a little bit of central London as an independent sovereign state.

It was a supreme piece of political make-believe to get round the Labour party's little difficulty of having neither a majority at Westminster nor any prospect of achieving one. Just as it is easy to forget how important a character Livingstone seemed to be, it is hard to remember that in the early 1980s people thought it was only the Liberals and the Social Democrats who could be regarded as an alternative government. No wonder there were plenty of people in the Labour party who thought it would make them credible again if only Livingstone could take his make-believe into parliamentary politics by becoming an MP. In fact, it was when he entered the House of Commons in 1987 that his influence started to decline. The Westminster club absorbed him fairly painlessly, as it has absorbed other radicals before him. The Gothic corridors have a salutary effect on revolutionaries and their fantasies. Boredom is more effective than bullets. The cheeky chap was not to be the one who would overturn the Iron Lady.

But the Livingstone story is still worth telling. Where did it start? Like many of the features of the Thatcher years, the Livingstone phenomenon had its roots in the Sixties, that decade when British society was up for grabs. Moral values, political values, economic values – everything was in the melting pot.

The 1960s began with Livingstone a pupil at Tulse Hill Comprehensive in South London. His father was a trawler-man (who had survived being torpedoed during the war), his mother a one-time acrobatic dancer who now supplemented the family income by working in a baker's shop or as an usherette in a cinema. His parents' meeting had been a war-time romance. Livingstone senior, on shore leave with two shipmates, had a few drinks and then attended the music hall where his future wife was performing. Messages passed between the sailors in the audience and the girls on the stage.

The son of this happy union of dancer and seaman was a slow developer. He failed the 11 plus. But he was lucky at Tulse Hill in his first-form master, Philip Hobsbawm, a distant relative of the Marxist historian Eric Hobsbawm who himself went on from school teaching to a notable university career. Hobsbawm did not go in for political indoctrination but he encouraged his classes to discuss current events. Livingstone learned the joys of debate. Put another way, in his own subsequent words about himself, 'I became an argumentative, cocky little brat.' Part of the cockiness consisted of poking fun at his father's fairly orthodox Tory views at the family dinner table.

By all accounts, however, Ken Livingstone's main teenage passion was not politics but natural history. His teenage hobby (to the delight of cartoonists in years to come) was collecting reptiles. Money earned on a newspaper round was spent on buying frogs, salamanders, snakes and at one time a baby alligator. His bent for natural history directed him towards his first job, as a lab technician in a cancer research centre, and it was there that his political antennae really began to twitch. He didn't much care for the hierarchical world of doctors. Nor did he like the way animals were used in experiments.

Protest and idealism were in the air in the early 1960s. In America, idealism crystallized in the election of President Kennedy and in the civil rights campaigns. In Britain, Harold Wilson talked about the white heat of the technological revolution. For the young, the world was at their feet. It is hard to understand the Thatcherite years without remembering those high hopes, followed by the disillusionment of the Seventies.

In 1966 Livingstone was one of the many young people of his generation who went off backpacking around the world. His motivations were various. Partly it was an interest in wild-life preservation and what was later to be called the environment. Partly it was the challenge of the developing countries of Africa and of 'racism'. He brushed against various idealistic young people in VSO and in Kennedy's Peace Corps. Meanwhile the Kennedy administration's idealism was beginning to hit trouble in Vietnam. Livingstone, on his travels, met a number of Vietnam draft dodgers.

He returned to London and seized on all the 'issue' politics of the late Sixties. He might well have decided to devote himself exclusively to the street politics of the times, for this was the heyday of the Vietnam demonstrations. Or he might have plunged himself into one or other of the one-issue organizations, like CND, that proliferated. Instead, he decided on a different course which was to have a significant impact on national politics. He decided to join the Labour party. Everybody else was leaving it. According to one's point of view, he breathed new life into the Labour party, or he prevented it from evolving in a sensible way.

His entry into the party at that time 'was one of the few recorded instances', he wrote later, 'of a rat climbing on board a sinking ship'. The party was ageing and creaking. London's local Labour parties tended to be in the hands of rusty machines run by a few old men who may have been Socialists with a capital S but were conservative with a small c. When Livingstone turned up at his first meeting of his local Labour ward he noted the delight on everyone's face – he was the first new member for a couple of years. He found himself put on committee after committee. 'My arrival', he said, 'had been rather like taking a bottle of gin into a room full of alcoholics. I was immediately passed round and consumed.' Ken Livingstone was always one for colourful metaphors.

He was soon an activist councillor in Lambeth, where he was contemptuous of the sitting Labour establishment, not least on their housing record. He was realistic enough to see that the Tories, when they took power, actually had a better housing policy. Active among those Lambeth Tories, incidentally, was another ambitious young man called John Major.

Meanwhile Livingstone decided he had to improve his earning capacity. He enrolled as a student at the Philippa Fawcett Teacher Training College. At college – 'a terrible place', he called it, 'full of vicars' daughters from the Home Counties' – he met one girl he liked, and married her. The arrangement seems to have been that she would earn a living for them by teaching so that he could pursue politics full-time, moving into the wider arena of the Greater London Council, and then, who knew where?

The marriage broke up, amicably. What really enabled him to become a full-time politician was not marriage but the local government reforms introduced by the Heath government, which had now replaced that of Harold Wilson. The reforms included provision for paying attendance allowances for councillors. It became possible for people of modest financial ambitions to make local politics a profession. This gave new hope to the Labour party. The British political centre of gravity was moving to the Right, or at least towards the Centre, after the brief aberration of national affection for Harold Wilson. The shift might have taken place more smoothly and more intelligently if the picture had not been distorted at the level of local politics, not just in Ken Livingstone's London but in various other major town halls around the country.

The age of the Loony Left in local politics was upon us. The difference with Ken Livingstone was that he came over to the public not as a loony but as a rather sensible chap. Most important of all, unlike the typical town hall socialist, he had a sense of humour. And he quickly grasped the important fact that power in politics goes to those who understand tactics rather than to those who think entirely in terms of dogma.

Getting control of the Greater London Council was entirely a matter of tactics. It was in any case a second prize. From local politics Livingstone had intended to get into Parliament in the general election of 1979. He was duly adopted as Labour candidate in Hampstead, which seemed a winnable seat, but had not foreseen the extent of the anti-Labour backlash which swept Mrs Thatcher to power in that year. Rejected by the Hampstead parliamentary electorate, he turned his attention seriously to the GLC.

He encouraged left-wingers to put themselves forward for selection as GLC candidates for the election due in 1981. Meanwhile he was careful not to offend middle-of-the-road Labour councillors, to whom he simply presented himself as a lively new broom who would make the council more effective. He devoted his considerable presentational skills to the Labour election manifesto, particularly to its proposals for London Transport. His transport theories had a sort of eccentric logic that appealed to many ordinary Londoners. If you brought down the fares of public transport, so the argument ran, more people would use it. People would see the sense of not commuting by car, and this would ease congestion.

As soon as the election took place, the old GLC Labour leadership was ditched. In the words of the headline writers, Red Ken had taken over. Confrontation ensued – confrontation with the minister in charge of local government (Michael Heseltine), with the courts which decided that his plans for subsidizing the travelling public were illegal, and with other London local authorities who knew they would have to pick up part of the bill. The battle drifted on for years. Eventually Mrs Thatcher decided on the ultimate solution: she abolished the GLC. Even in that process, Red Ken managed to have, if not the last, certainly the penultimate laugh. As the abolition legislation ground through Parliament he found himself in unlikely alliance with a minority of Conservative peers who disliked the legislation more than they disliked Red Ken. Some of them had constitutional scruples. Some of them just did not like the Prime Minister and found the Bill as good a pretext as any for creating trouble for her.

The Thatcher years ended with Ken Livingstone's old headquarters at County Hall standing empty and awaiting 'redevelopment', with his kind of socialism even less likely to win acceptance from the public at large, and with the state of London Transport a source of even greater irritation to the public.

Over on the Westminster side of the river it was a bleak time for Ken Livingstone. He did not fit into the new, sanitized Labour party which was hoping to win the 1992 election. Electors were supposed to prefer men in suits with roses in their buttonholes. Ken was a reminder of the days when the party was run from bedsitters by men in pullovers.

The climax of the 1992 Labour campaign, a showbiz extravaganza at Sheffield, had all the right people, sleek and smooth, disporting themselves on the stage for the TV cameras. Many Tories, at that delicate stage in what was proving to be a nervewracking campaign, were openly jealous. Ken was not invited to Sheffield. Indeed, he remarked bitterly, he hadn't been invited to *anything* for years. He was rather rude about Neil Kinnock: if the media were saying (as they were) how skilful Neil was, there must be something seriously amiss.

Anti-leadership Labour MPs usually complain that the party establishment is too timid to hit the rich hard enough. Ken introduced a twist to that argument. The people who drew up Labour's tax proposals in 1992 didn't know the facts of life in inner London. Twenty thousand a year – that wasn't riches. It was the going rate for his working-class constituents.

After the election, when Neil resigned the leadership, Ken offered himself for the job but didn't get over the initial hurdle of finding fifty-five MPs to back him. He grumbled about the unions who had stitched it all up. 'If we had a primaries system operating here,' he said, 'I'd be totally confident of my ability to win.' He may have been right.

8

Good, honest, anarchic fun
ANITA RODDICK

*It's the power of money, and if you can apply that money to good,
so much the bloody better.*

ANITA RODDICK

THE PICTURE often painted of Anita Roddick, of 'Body Shop' fame, is of a slightly wacky, Green feminist who happens to have made a lot of money along the way. There is an element of truth in that, but perhaps it puts her character upside down.

Anita Roddick rose to power and influence at almost precisely the same time as Margaret Thatcher did – the late Seventies and early Eighties. There is indeed an interesting similarity between their respective childhoods, although in one case the family background was Italian Catholic immigrant and in the other Methodist English. Both grew up in shops where the children were expected to work behind the counter. Anita Roddick's parents ran a seaside café where, she has put on record, 'the work ethic was extremely strong'. The incentive to work grew stronger after her father died when she was 10.

She was a bright, dedicated scholar at school, and – apparently because she was fascinated by the English language, spoken as well as written – she tried to enter drama school. Failing that, she went to teacher training college and evidently turned out to be a gifted, if unconventional, teacher.

Britain had now entered the Swinging Sixties, and Anita was into all the fashionable do-goodery – CND, Shelter, the lot. She liked to claim that at one time she was involved in a plan to take over the empty Centre Point building. In common with plenty of girls of her generation, she decided that there was a lot of the hippy in her makeup, and went off to bum round the world with a boyfriend.

The Third World fascinated her, and the Body Shop concept began to take shape, although she may not have realized it at the time. In primitive corners of the globe she was intrigued to watch women caring for their bodies without expensive potions in expensive bottles. In Morocco she watched them wash their hair in a special kind of mud. In Tahiti they cleansed their skin with cocoa butter.

She never lost her respect for the idealism of the Sixties. 'I just think', she was to observe later, 'the only reason it wasn't effective in terms of social change was because none of us had the strength of economics.' The 'strength of economics' emerged when eventually she returned home to Little-hampton in Sussex, where the parental café had been. Enter Gordon Roddick. Their courtship, she likes to say, lasted all of four and a half minutes. They became business partners as well as husband and wife.

There was something of the hippy in Gordon too (he was a frustrated novelist) but between them the Roddick team had a firm grasp of the work ethic. They also took the view, which was still a rather unfashionable one in the Britain of the Sixties and Seventies, that there is nothing to be ashamed of in making money. They started a wholefood restaurant, but market forces seemed to indicate that their future did not lie there.

The restaurant was a success, but exhausted them. Anita, who now had two young children to look after, decided that she would prefer a nine-to-five job; Gordon decided to recharge his batteries by going off on a horseback trek from

Argentina to New York. Anita looked for premises to start a little shop.

The first Body Shop was squeezed between two funeral parlours in Brighton. According to Roddick folklore, the name 'Body Shop' was devised partly because the modest width of the shop frontage limited the number of letters that could be written above the shop window. But Anita, with her delight in the whimsical byways of the English language, had had a soft spot for the words 'Body Shop' ever since she had noted that this was how car body repairers described their premises in America. Her neighbours the funeral undertakers were less than enchanted to find themselves next door to a Body Shop, and made disapproving noises. At once Anita was on the 'phone to the local newspaper, disguising her voice with a handkerchief over the mouthpiece, to say that local businessmen were 'trying to stop a poor little housewife struggling to set up a face-cream shop'. It was the first of many Roddick exercises in getting free publicity. Customers came, out of curiosity, and kept coming because they liked what she was selling.

Much of the ambience of the Body Shop grew out of trivial circumstances. The colour of the famous decor, dark green, was chosen not because of the significance of Green-ness, which did not become fashionable till later, but because it was the only colour that would hide the damp patches.

Meanwhile Gordon returned from his expedition on horseback to take over the backroom planning for the business and do the financial homework. Anita developed her product range, added the magic of her own dynamic personality and made sure that the name Body Shop was always in the news. The rest of the story is, as they say, history. The first shop had opened in March 1976: by the end of the Eighties, Body Shops spanned the globe and the Roddicks were reckoned to be personally worth more than £100 million. The significant growth had taken place during the very years, the early

Eighties, when an economic blizzard was sweeping through British industry. In other words, Body Shops were opening while factories were closing.

Part of the driving motivation for Anita Roddick was that the money could be used for good works. Those foot rollers on her shelves that do wonders for your nerve endings when you exercise your soles on them – they were made in 'Boys' Towns' in southern India, run on the most enlightened lines. She helped to set up a paper-making plant in Tibet. A soap factory was deliberately sited in the impoverished outskirts of Glasgow, with a proportion of the profits being handed over to the community.

The Green ethic – no animal testing of cosmetics, no whale oils, everything ecologically sound, and a generally benevolent philosophy – was very 1980s. It also appealed to her principles to sell her creams, lotions and potions in very basic containers, with no fancy wrappers, whereas in the traditional cosmetics industry – 'run by men', she would say briskly – 'the major produce is garbage'. She doesn't believe in fashionable marketing hype – no pictures of glamorous women, and indeed no advertising. She calculated that this was the no-nonsense approach that would appeal to the kind of 1980s woman who was irritated at the thought of paying more for the bottle and the wrapping than she paid for the stuff she was actually going to smear on her face.

But the real significance of the Body Shop phenomenon was that it provided a textbook example of a business technique that could be successful in the 1980s, while so many traditional companies were going to the wall. Consider these features of the Roddick business:

Although it was contemptuous of marketing hype, Body Shop, to use modern management jargon, was 'market driven' – that is, it identified a real demand, from real people, for something that those people were prepared to pay for.

It was not ashamed of exploiting the fact that people are prepared to pay money for things that would once have been thought of as inessential fripperies.

It allowed the public to cock a snook at the old commercial establishment: for women buying face creams, it had often, in the past, been a case of Boots or nothing; now there was an exciting alternative on offer – from a woman who clearly didn't give a damn if she offended the establishment.

The business style was very personal – the old concept of the 'entrepreneur' was being revived.

But this was a new type of entrepreneur: quite apart from being a woman, Anita Roddick was not in the mould of the people whom the British, in days gone by, had expected to be running a business of this magnitude.

Although the Body Shop did not spend money on advertising, the company attached major emphasis to public and press relations: when Body Shop was launched in the United States it contrived to earn the accolade of an article in *Life* magazine.

All these were pointers to the new entrepreneurialism. Body Shop was in fact a doubly entrepreneurial organization – most individual Body Shops were independent businesses run by franchise-holders. Franchising has had mixed fortunes as a commercial technique in the UK, but appears to have been a great success in this case. Because the original concept was so soundly based, the demand for franchises was big enough for the Roddicks to choose from among the business élite to represent Body Shop standards around the country and around the world.

So the Body Shop franchise pattern fitted the Thatcherite industrial philosophy of the 1980s – insofar as the government of the 1980s had such a strategy. Many of Britain's big companies, with their ponderous managerial hierarchies, taken for granted as the norm in the Sixties and Seventies, were in decline. Their place would be taken – this was the theory of the economic gurus whose views carried weight in Downing Street – by a new breed of small, owner-managed businesses, run by a new breed of lean and hungry entrepreneurs.

Was it really necessary for so many employees of the old-established big firms to be thrown out of work under the pressure of monetarist logic? Can enough new small businesses be created to take their place? We still await answers to these questions. But there have certainly been examples of interesting newcomers on the business scene – many of them started, indeed, with redundancy money paid out to people fleeing from the industrial wasteland of the early 1980s.

The Body Shop is an outstanding example of a small business that grew into a big one, and there are others. The Roddicks belonged to one of the new privileged classes of the 1980s: the 'USM millionaires'. In other words, they were able to expand their company because they could go to the Unlisted Securities Market. That market came into existence only in 1980. Before then, while it had been possible for big, established companies seeking to raise extra capital to go to the Stock Exchange, smaller companies, unknown to the City, had problems. The USM brought together the riches and expertise of the City (where a new, more entrepreneurial type of operator was coming to the fore) and the Roddick-type entrepreneurs in unfashionable places like Brighton.

The Roddicks were approached, at quite an early stage in their company's history, by a City operator called Brod Munroe Wilson, who had once worked for Hill Samuel but had now set up on his own. He had become aware of a Body Shop that had appeared in the City itself, had observed that it always seemed to be full of customers, and sensed that this was precisely the sort of embryo commercial empire for which the USM had been created. 'How would you like to be millionaires?' he asked the Roddicks. Their answer appears to have been 'Not particularly, thank you.'

But the fact that they had been noticed by somebody in the City *did* interest them. They may not have been greedy for cash, but they were ambitious for their company. At that time their chain of shops was only just starting to grow, and they were discovering that they had a problem in finding good high street sites, in competition with better known chains, because their company was not taken seriously. They were certainly taken seriously when they floated on the USM in 1984: a million shares were offered, priced at 95p; that same afternoon, the price went up to 160p.

The financial world was changing rapidly in the 1980s in all sorts of ways which meant that unexpected people had to be taken seriously. Writing in the *Financial Times* in 1988, one commentator, John Lloyd, put it thus:

> Britain is no longer run by an Establishment. In its place is a Disestablishment comprising the men and women whose values, assumptions are those of outsiders. Often they still perceive themselves as outsiders, radicals, anti-Establishment figures but that is increasingly a pose.
>
> They have successfully dethroned much, though not all, of the old Establishment and in many crucial centres of power have taken its place.

The men and women of the Disestablishment vary considerably in character. Anita Roddick is one of the more likeable, perhaps simply because she seems to enjoy her (very profitable) work so much. What she has created, she once said, is 'an international network of good, honest, anarchic fun'.

9

Market economics the civilized way

TIM WATERSTONE

THE TALE of Tim Waterstone is one of the *nicest* stories of the 1980s. He is a very nice man and he is a businessman who believes that work ought to be fun. One business school student writing a thesis on the Waterstone success story decided to entitle it 'Management by Joy'.

When a pleasant man makes a lot of money it gives us all a warm glow. Waterstone made his money, moreover, in the most respectable of trades, bookselling. And he did it through a determination to please his customers, and to provide congenial conditions for his staff. There is another part of the story that creates a warm glow. It all began when he was sacked by his former employers, the bookselling giant, W. H. Smith: he bounced back from that misfortune by going off to make a fortune on his own. Altogether, a very moral tale. One has the feeling about Waterstone, who looks rather like a vicar of the more agreeable sort, that he has a healthy working relationship with Somebody up there.

As with a lot of the more interesting people who scaled the heights in British life in the past, there is a link with the Indian Raj. His father was chairman of a tea company, and

Waterstone started his career in India, before becoming a management trainee at Allied Breweries, which he regarded as one of the more enlightened British employers of the time. For ten years he was marketing manager of Allied's wines and spirits division, then joined W. H. Smith, to run its book distribution business. It seemed a good move – he was a book lover, and he was now an experienced marketing man. In fact, the highly individualistic Waterstone did not fit into the hierarchy of a big company, and when an attempt to take Smith's into the American market went wrong, his head was on the block.

He lost his job just when a lot of other people were losing their jobs too – in 1981. He had six children to support, and a house which at that point, it emerged, was subsiding and needed £30,000 worth of work done on it. There were no satisfactory jobs on offer. He woke up one morning realizing that he had to go it alone. He thus qualifies as one of the New Entrepreneurs of the Thatcher era, who set up their own businesses because, with much of the old corporate world apparently collapsing about their ears in the early Eighties, they had no option.

In setting up the Waterstone bookstores, in one respect at least he had no difficulty in fitting in with the fashionable market economics of the Thatcherite times: he believed in giving the market what it wants – the businessman must study what people want, and then make sure he provides the highest quality of service in meeting their demands. What did his potential customers want? He was convinced, contrary to much accepted wisdom about the philistinism of the British, that we do actually want to buy books, good books, and would buy more of them if we were given the chance.

Waterstone subscribed to the old American maxim about retailing, that there are only three things which determine whether a store is successful: location, location and location. So it was policy for Waterstone shops to be set up in good shopping sites. 'It's nonsense to tuck bookshops away,' he said. 'They are as much retail as fast food or shoes.'

Good sites meant high rents, and, to justify the cost, the space he rented was made to work hard: he filled his shops with twice as many books per square foot as the ordinary bookshop. An average Waterstone shop carried 60,000 titles, as against 5,000–10,000 in some of his rivals. 'This is absolutely first-division retailing,' he would say, 'sales of £300 per square foot. Much higher than Next.'

There was another way he made his shops work hard. With memories of New York bookstores, he opened his shops in the evening. A visit to a bookshop could be a social occasion. He would point proudly, on a bleak winter's evening, to browsers, sometimes whole family groups, 'absorbed in the world of books'. When a customer chatted to a sales assistant, he felt it ought to be an enjoyable and instructive experience. His policy was to have well-informed staff, initially all graduates. 'There was such extreme demoralization in the book trade', he recalled, 'that the standard of retail staff had been allowed to drift down to a staggering low.'

When he planned the Waterstone concept, as he modestly explained in later years, he was 'not clever enough to see the problems'. But he found that his ideas, backed with his experience, enabled him to raise the necessary capital, if not from the most conventional sources. That canny old Scottish publishing group, D. C. Thomson, came up with a substantial chunk of funds. So did a number of venture-capital houses, including 3i (Investors in Industry). Most interesting, and in tune with the times, a large number of small investors put up modest sums under the Business Expansion Scheme. All these people, like Waterstone himself, were to see a very good return on their money.

Throughout the 1980s, Waterstone shops kept appearing around the country. By 1988 there were 31 of them, with 550 staff and a turnover of £32 million. In the space of seven years, Waterstone had revolutionized the face of British bookselling and revitalized hardback publishing, because existing booksellers found themselves obliged to raise standards too. The revolution had an impact on publishers, who felt able to become that much more 'literary' in their commercial strategy. Even poetry, it was said, could be made to sell.

There was something of the missionary in the man. Of Anglo-Catholic leanings, he liked to pray on his daily journey (by foot) to work. He belonged to one of the great traditions of Victorian entrepreneurialism, when the Bible and the cash book lay side by side. Work ethics ought to be a source not only of profits but also of personal satisfaction – and fun – for everyone.

Waterstone had no doubts about the importance of profits, and responsibility for profits was devolved to branch managers. They decided what to stock. They picked their own staff. 'We give responsibility very early, employ none but bright people, and give them the joy of building their own businesses . . . It's all self-help, self-start, self-knowledge.'

But would the profits be big enough to justify the levels of service he was ambitious to provide? In the eyes of many pundits of the trade, profitability depended, and depends, on the famous, or notorious, Net Book Agreement. The NBA is the last remnant of the host of gentlemanly restrictive practices which once ensured that British businessmen did not actually have to compete with one another. Long before the zealots of Thatcherism came along, it was recognized that they had to go. One by one, the fences have given way to market economics. Even lawyers nowadays are allowed to tender for work and to undercut their colleagues at the other end of the high street.

The argument for the survival of the NBA is that selling books is a different matter from selling cornflakes or doing the conveyancing on a house sale. Waterstone, as we have seen, argued that bookselling is just like any other retailing, but he nevertheless supported the NBA. The way it works is that booksellers do not undercut each other, even on bestsellers which practically sell themselves. In theory, if the bookseller can thus make a good profit on popular books, he is more likely to have the financial security that will enable him to provide a good service to the discerning book-buyer – he will have time to answer inquiries, and be able to carry a broad stock of less popular titles. As Waterstone put it, 'I don't want to see St Augustine's Confessions double in price; I want to see it kept at £3.95 in Penguin Classics.'

But one suspects that Tim Waterstone felt that the old school of booksellers could have done a lot more, with their profits from the high mark-up provided by the NBA, to provide a better service. As we all know, many of the traditional high-quality booksellers that were to be found around the country in the 1970s were splendid shops, run on the most worthy principles, but they often suffered, like too much of British industry at the time, from a lack of commercial drive.

Waterstone's strategy was to bridge the obvious gap between these worthy establishments and the big boys of the book retailing trade, notably Smith's. An ambience of old-fashioned worthiness was not what the new book-buying classes wanted. Although they were interested in serious reading, they saw no reason why book-buying should be an austere experience. There was no reason to put on a hair shirt to buy St Augustine. Tim Waterstone, although the least glitzy of men, craftily made sure that his shops, stacked to the ceiling with stock though they might be, conveyed an impression of comfortable, relaxed well-being, even hedonism. The interior designers were brought in. Clever things were done with ox-blood and black. He knew he was dealing with a public who had come to associate shopping with theatrical lights and classical music.

He knew, too, that it was fair game to catch them young. 'My children', he would explain, 'like to go to Smith's on a Saturday morning to buy elephant-shaped erasers, colouring kits and artists' materials. I thought: why don't we do this with much more style, move it upmarket?' So were born Young Waterstones, but none of them survived into adolescence.

By the end of the 1980s, he had achieved an interesting double. He featured in all the lists of case studies of the Thatcher Enterprise Revolution. He also held a place of honour among Britain's intellectuals for breathing new life into the concept of civilized people building up their own libraries. Then in 1989, in the eyes of many of the intellectual establishment, he blotted his copy book – by rejoining the fold of W. H. Smith.

His reasons for doing so were largely technical. His business had reached the stage where it needed a broader financial base. It would have been appropriate to float on the stock market, but in the late Eighties flotation was not the attractive option it once had been. There was also the challenge of the threatened ending of the Net Book Agreement. In any event, he negotiated a merger with Sherratt & Hughes, the specialist subsidiary of Smith's, which was one of his main competitors. The agreement was that he would run the joint operation for four years. Apart from anything else, he said, it meant greater security for his staff.

Whatever the future, he had earned a place in the history of the 1980s. Waterstone bookshops made a major contribution to the cultural life of his country. And he proved that market economics can work that much better when they are in the hands of civilized men. He sold Waterstone's for £40 million; his share came to £9 million.

10

How to succeed in business

MICHAEL ASHCROFT

'GROWTH' WAS one of the buzz words of the Thatcher years. In business-speak, there are two ways to make a company grow: organic growth and growth by acquisition. Organic growth means building more plant or machinery, selling more widgets, manufacturing your widgets more efficiently. On the other hand, you can improve your balance sheet by making a shrewd buy of somebody else's company which is good at making widgets. That is growth by acquisition, growth by dextrous deals.

The 1980s were a decade of deal-making. A whole generation of young people were trained in the City, during 'Big Bang' and the yuppie revolution, in the art of the deal. It was part of the Eighties culture. Some of us can remember an earlier culture when ambitious young Britons were schooled in the 'Everest' ethos – you climbed a mountain because it was *there*. Now, ambitious young men and women scanned the horizon for opportunities for a 'good deal', and aspired to clinch it because it was there. Whether the completed deal increased the sum total of human happiness didn't matter. It was deal-making *per se* that was the challenge. It raised the adrenalin. It was the fun thing to do and the glamorous thing to do. It earned admiring glances from the opposite sex. It was living dangerously. It could also mean living very profitably.

Of the deal-makers on an heroic scale, a name to conjure with was that of Michael Ashcroft. 'Business', he once said, 'is like endless war games.' Changing the metaphor, he is on record as stating that his own business 'is marginally more exciting than an orgasm'. Clever deal-making took the value of his company, ADT Group plc, up to the £2 billion mark.

The rise of Michael Ashcroft was one of the success stories of Margaret Thatcher's regime. Coincidentally, by the time she was replaced by John Major, the magic had gone out of the Ashcroft name. He himself seemed to be in no doubt that his business methods mirrored all that was most dynamic in Conservative policy in the 1980s. Or perhaps he would have put it the other way round.

The Conservative party was more cautious in returning the compliment, notwithstanding the friendship that developed between him and Denis Thatcher. Ashcroft had hoped to become Conservative party treasurer. The party thought differently – but welcomed his financial generosity to it. It was even prepared to use him as a guarantor for its overdraft. He was generous, too, to various causes close to Tory hearts. He found a sizeable proportion of the funds for the setting up of a City Technology College in Wandsworth, that London showplace of the new model Toryism.

All these activities were mere spin-offs from his real skills of innovation, which lay in acquiring or disposing of company shares. Michael Ashcroft symbolized as much as any one man the revolution that took place in the Square Mile in the 1980s. He stood for the new guard taking over from the old in the City. His name could be added to the long list of sharp young men who have felt they are cold-shouldered in the City because they are not out of the top drawer.

Even by 1979, of course, the days were long past when the

City was run wholly by gents. By the time Michael came on the scene, power lay very much in the hands of men, and even some women, out of middle and lower drawers. Part of the Ashcroft mythology which grew up was that his determination to get to the top reflected how he had been patronized by the City establishment. But his background was scarcely working-class. He was brought up as an ex-pat, in what was still the colonial empire. His father was posted to British Honduras (now Belize) as Principal Auditor – which meant, incidentally, that reading columns of figures was in the blood. (Belize was later to honour Michael by making him its ambassador to the European Community.)

When the family returned home he joined the sixth form of Maidenhead Royal Grammar School. From there he went into a management training scheme at Rothman's and worked for a time for the cleaning company Pritchard Services. He set himself up as a consultant and the story is that he took a copy of Yellow Pages and simply phoned round offering his services.

The fact that he had been at a grammar school, albeit only for a year or two, was widely supposed to have had immense significance when he found himself among the City's public schoolboys. When eventually he was in a position to buy and sell people, so the story goes, instead of turning up to sign the completion of a deal, he would send his chauffeur with a power of attorney to sign for him. It was not a gesture that was highly appreciated.

So he was yet another of the grammar-school boys who were taking over from the public schoolboys in the 1970s and '80s. In that, at least, he mirrored the political revolution of the 1980s in which the top-drawer Tories were given their come-uppance. His attitude to the establishment was that if you can't join it you lick it.

In the new meritocratic City, his talents were unquestionable. He had the kind of brain that takes on board the detail of a score of balance sheets simultaneously, and the intricacies of complicated cross-holdings of shares. He dipped into company reports for relaxation as other men read Agatha Christie. On his honeymoon, apparently, he took the latest Finance Act with him to read. It was said he acquired holdings in literally thousands of quoted companies simply to give him access to their annual reports. Nobody could accuse the Michael Ashcrofts of the new City of not doing their homework, in a way that some of their predecessors had been too casual to do. In that, too, there was a parallel with what happened as the new men took over from the old men in the Tory party.

The management training was useful, but it was not so much management as ownership that interested him. In those days it was possible to identify companies that could be made vastly more profitable by applying some fairly simple management rules. You bought one, turned it round and sold it on. After you had made your first million, subsequent millions were that much easier. He had the satisfaction of taking over his old employers, Pritchards.

The creation of his empire was largely a one-man achievement. He was never a great team player. He masterminded every detail of a deal. It began when he persuaded a bank to lend him enough money to buy an inexpensive cleaning company. Five years later he sold it, to Reckitt and Colman, for £1.3 million. Now in his early thirties, he possessed enough working capital to take on the City.

He did the acquisition trick again, buying an underperforming company called Hawley, concerned mainly with camping equipment, and making it highly profitable. (In dealmaking, it often doesn't matter what the company does; it is the numbers on the balance sheet that are important.) Things then seemed to happen very quickly indeed. The deals spiralled and became more complex. They also crossed the Atlantic, to the United States, Canada and Central America. ADT, which became his main vehicle, was a Bermuda-based company supplying security systems, which he bought in 1984.

There were dawn raids and boardroom coups. The list of products and services his companies were involved in got longer and longer – bedroom furniture, amusement machines, electronic surveillance equipment, car auctions. There was even a firm that converted Ford Granadas into hearses or armoured cars.

Fairly early on, knowledgeable people in the City marked their card with the name Ashcroft. To the wider public he was unknown until he joined the board of Miss World. Like other rich, ambitious men, he had been lured by the glitter of show business. At the upmarket end of show business, he sponsored the London City Ballet.

It was the ballet connection that brought social kudos. Patron of the London City Ballet was the Princess of Wales. The Ashcroft face – boyish, bespectacled, thrusting – which had become increasingly familiar on the City pages of the serious newspapers, now appeared on the gossip pages of the tabloids. Money, royalty, *arrivisme* . . . But there was another quality. Gossip columnists, in that era of affluence, were not slow to apply one of the favoured words of the period: *naff*. If a yacht (like Ashcroft's) was too big, too showy, it was naff. The same applied to Rolls-Royces (his was sky blue) and to Cartier watches. When, entertaining the Princess of Wales, he wore a silver bow tie with his dinner jacket, the naffness screamed out. To the delight of the media, he even persuaded the Princess to go dog-racing at Wembley in aid of a good cause.

There was no shortage of admirers in the enterprise years of the Eighties. In 1983 he placed an advertisement in the *Financial Times* for two executives to join him. 'The pace and requirements will be extremely demanding and by normal criteria unreasonable,' it said. Applicants had to be prepared to spend up to twenty-four hours a day, seven days a week, on projects anywhere in the UK or US. The response, he reported, was enormous.

He told his critics that they didn't understand him. His methods were, indeed, hard for slower minds to understand. It was sometimes difficult to tell how much his alienation from the City establishment was due to his resentment of them and how much to their fear that he might be brighter than they were. 'There are two things the average Brit dislikes,' he once said. 'One is failure, the other is success.'

He also understood another idiosyncrasy of the City down the centuries. They expect people who have made a large fortune to disburse some of it, and many philanthropists direct their public service into areas associated with their business. Michael, who earned a substantial part of his money from security systems, established what came to be known as the 'Crimestoppers' Movement' – the Community Action Trust.

All these excellent services to the national good of the British people were somewhat shadowed by the fact that he found it convenient to base many of his business interests outside British territorial control. The Thatcher years had done much to make London a good centre for international business operations. But places like Bermuda could still be more attractive. Michael Ashcroft's own preferred home became Florida.

The heyday of the Ashcroft empire was the 1980s. By the end of the decade, the glitter of the whizzkids began to look tarnished. Things were not helped by some high-profile scandals, including Blue Arrow. Ashcroft was mentioned, but not implicated. Allegations were made about share dealings in ADT. Writs flew. Michael, master of the transatlantic deal, discovered the truth of the Wall Street dictum, 'Don't hesitate, litigate – then negotiate.' The beginning of the 1990s was a time when the City had to take a long hard look at what it had admired in the Eighties, and that included Michael Ashcroft.

Ashcroft's extra-territorial dimension was one reason why the Conservative party felt it inappropriate to give him the kind of job he would have liked. All appearances somewhat to the contrary, Michael Ashcroft was a man who wanted to be loved. That alone made him slightly different from some Thatcherites.

11

Mr Chairman
SIR JOHN CUCKNEY

For a few brief days in January 1986 – an unseasonably mild January as it will be remembered – it seemed as if the unsinkable SS *Thatcher* had come into contact with the iceberg that would be too much for her. The hull was indeed badly holed, but only above the waterline. Nevertheless, the Westland crisis of 1986 stands out as a political turning point of the Thatcher years. Two lesser vessels were sunk, though not without trace: Michael Heseltine and Leon Brittan. Aboard the flagship, the crew heaved a sigh of relief, but were never quite so confident again.

When political drama builds up on the scale of Westland, it does not matter what precisely triggers it off. In this case it was helicopters. If it hadn't been helicopters, it might well have been something else that caused Michael Heseltine to storm out of the Cabinet and into Downing Street that January. But the story of Westland itself, a rather small company with rather large problems, is worth examining because it contains a lot of what was happening in British industry in the Thatcher years.

That brings us to the key figure of Sir John Cuckney.

Cuckney, behind the scenes, was one of the most important people in the political drama. He was not himself a politician. He was chairman of Westland. At one time or another, it sometimes seemed, he had been chairman of practically *everything*. British public life has always had a way of producing men clearly intended by the Almighty to be chairmen. Different periods of history have called for different philosophies about how the job should be done. By the 1980s, John Cuckney seemed to epitomize the kind of chairmanship that fitted the needs of the Thatcherite era. He was determined. He was an activist. He had no time for the argument that you should do this, or not do that, simply because that is the way things have always been.

Moreover, he looked the part. If there had ever been a time in the 1970s or '80s when the demand in the City or in Westminster for John Cuckney as a chairman dried up – which never seemed likely – he could have switched careers and taken on a lucrative succession of film appearances in a certain type of supporting role. He had the authoritative figure that carries a well-cut suit to perfection and that looks right for stepping out of a limousine, smiling briefly at the waiting photographers and sweeping up the steps to take command of a meeting that is going to put the world to rights. His features always exuded businesslike goodwill, immense urbanity and intelligence, but were clearly those of a man who never puts up with any nonsense.

In a sense, he had the air of belonging to the good old days when Britain was run by an Establishment. But, you may ask, had Mrs Thatcher not abolished the Establishment? This is partly what makes John Cuckney so interesting. He never fitted into a stereotype.

For a man who eventually seemed so much at home in the City, there was something enigmatic about him. He had come to the world of finance comparatively late in life. His family background was military. His father, a First World War pilot, was an air vice-marshal. The school chosen for him – Shrewsbury – is one which has produced its fair share of slightly offbeat members of the Establishment (including, ironically enough, Michael Heseltine, Richard Ingrams, Willie Rushton and the author).

Cuckney started studying medicine at St Andrews, then went off to war service. Back at St Andrews he switched from medicine to history and economics – he explained that he had seen too much of hospitals as a soldier to relish the idea of becoming a doctor. Other aspects of Army service apparently held more interest for him, for his first civilian job was, so to speak, military. In the words of his entry in *Who's Who*, he was on 'attachment to War Office (Civil Asst., Gen. Staff) until 1957'. We all know what *that* means.

Some light on this stage of his career was eventually to be provided by the publication of *Spycatcher*, Peter Wright's exposé of British counter-intelligence methods during the Cold War. For what it is worth, Wright seems to have felt that Cuckney was not a typical MI5 *apparatchik* – he was always his own man, with interests beyond the dark world of spying and counter-spying. And he dressed better than most of Wright's colleagues.

So Cuckney's apprenticeship in the City did not begin until he was well into his thirties. Soon he was working for Lazards. Then he moved, quietly but firmly, into public life. The late 1960s and the '70s were the period when British governments, Labour and Conservative, were struggling to find the right dividing line between the public and private sectors of industry. In this grey area where the State and private enterprise come face to face, Cuckney found a niche for his City talents.

In 1970 the Heath government appointed him chairman of the Mersey Docks and Harbour Board, which was facing insolvency. He restructured its finances and restored it to viability. His initial introduction to the complexities of government transport policy had in fact been under a Labour government – Barbara Castle took him into the Transport Minister's railway policy review committee in 1966.

105

From the Mersey Docks, he went on to become chief executive of the Property Services Agency, set up to bring the government's various property-owning and management activities under businesslike control. Next – this was under a Labour government again – he was brought in to sort out the mess into which the Crown Agents had got themselves by indulging in risky financial transactions at the time of the troubles in the secondary banking sector. From that Cuckney went on to the Port of London Authority, where he tried to do what he had done for the Mersey Docks but resigned when the Callaghan government refused to accept the logic of closing the Royal Docks.

He was now regarded as an outstandingly 'safe pair of hands' to be trusted in financial disasters, and his acceptance as such was marked with a knighthood from the Labour government. He developed a reputation not only for determination but also for utter integrity in his business dealings. His skills seemed to be most relevant when the need was to bring financial sanity, and free-market economics, into Civil Service-type situations. But by the late 1970s any rapport he had had with Labour governments must have been exhausted. By that time, the whole of British industry seemed to be exhausted too. The 'British disease' was beginning to look terminal.

The Thatcher government, when it came to power in 1979, decided the solution was to turn its back on the idea of trying to find a role for Whitehall in company boardroom decision-making. The State's job was to get the monetary totals right: after that it was up to companies to work out their own salvation.

For the next few years, it seemed that many of Britain's companies were not going to make it. The fact that there happened to be a world recession in the early 1980s did not help. In two years, the unemployment rate rose to 11 per cent, and output fell by about 6 per cent. In boardrooms, hard decisions had to be taken. It was against that gloomy backcloth that Cuckney turned himself into a company chairman *par excellence*. In 1978 he had become chairman of the troubled Thomas Cook (another example of a hybrid private-public enterprise operation). He now became chairman of Brooke Bond and of John Brown plc (which he saved from imminent collapse), and a director of various other public companies. Former medical student that he was, he now found himself referred to by newspaper headline writers as a 'company doctor' who never lost a patient. It was a description he disliked, but companies certainly tended to have much healthier balance sheets after the arrival of Cuckney than before.

In contrast to other big names in the corporate world, he never claimed to be a great administrator – he never aspired to the now fashionable title adopted by a certain type of tycoon, 'chairman and chief executive'. He was a great believer in the value of the non-executive director as a source of useful experience in a boardroom. Part of his own value to any one company, he believed, was that he had other interests outside it. 'Probably the most common problem I find in a company', he once said, 'is a failure to adapt to a changing marketplace. It's amazing how insular companies can become.'

While a company's chief executive must necessarily concentrate on what is going on inside the company, the value of the chairman is to cast his eyes outside. Despite being a very private man, or perhaps even because he was such a private man, Cuckney as a company chairman was extremely conscious of the importance of public relations – relations with governmental bodies, with the community at large and, of course, with the company's shareholders. This last was to be a vital consideration during the Westland episode.

Cuckney was an advocate of the 'enterprise revolution' which took place during the Thatcher years, and was incidentally much better qualified to talk about it than some of the zealots around the Prime Minister. Unlike them, he had actually presided over companies that made things happen in the real world.

In due course he added the chairmanships of 3i (Investors in Industry) and of Royal Insurance to the list. He had a particular affection for the venture-capital group 3i, which he saw as symbolizing much of what was best in the enterprise revolution: 3i's function was to put money behind entrepreneurial businesses, mainly smaller companies, which were growing during the 1980s to fill some of the gaps left when big companies were forced to pull out of areas where they were simply not efficient enough to compete. Under Thatcher the corporate character of British industry was changing, usually involuntarily and all too often painfully. How did this apply to the Westland helicopter company?

Westland was in many ways a very British institution, centred in that archetypal English town, Yeovil, in Somerset. It was good at making military helicopters, but its awareness of the realities of the marketplace was open to question. Relying on military orders, it had not worried overmuch about market economics. There had been an unhappy attempt to convert a military design into a civilian helicopter for which it was assumed there would be a massive demand in the United States, for taxi-ing people to airports from city centres. When one of these converted W30 Westland helicopters made an embarrassing forced landing, such enthusiasm as there had ever been for the helicopter taxi evaporated quickly. Moreover, nobody seems to have calculated the full extent of opposition from the environmental lobby to helicopters in city centres. It was a classic case of what Cuckney called 'insularity'. By 1985 the Westland company was on the verge of financial failure. Under the aegis of the Bank of England, concerned at the exposure of Westland's bankers, Cuckney took over as chairman.

According to the strict rules of Thatcherism, the issue should have been simple: Westland would have to be made profitable or be taken over by a different management able to turn it round. The company had a 'sponsor department' in Whitehall – Leon Brittan's Department of Trade and Industry – but the days were past when sponsor departments picked up the tab to prevent the receivers from being called in to a failing company.

In fact, of course, the issue was not as simple as that. Westland could scarcely be said to operate in a free market. The company featured in the strategic plans of the Department of Defence, presided over by Michael Heseltine. It depended on government orders, and in defence contracts there are considerations which override commercial calculations.

Sir John Cuckney understood all this as well as anyone. Although his devotion to the free-enterprise cause was not in question when he took over as Westland's chairman, he had no objections in principle to some kind of government assistance to keep the special skills of the Westland company intact for the national good. However, as he was to put it in January 1986, at the height of the crisis:

A view had been taken by the government that it was to be treated as a private sector problem entirely. Having been told that the company is on its own, there's no point in whingeing about it. One has to get on and deal with it.

But then the goal posts were moved again, at least by one part of the government. A very high-profile interventionist role was adopted which is certainly confusing for the company and its employees.

There speaks the simple industrialist fed up with the shenanigans of politicians. Actually, Cuckney's way of 'getting on and dealing with it' revealed considerable political as well as financial skill. Perhaps because the years of 'attachment to War Office' had toughened his antennae, he proved that he was at least as sharp as the politicians when it came to fighting his corner.

Having decided that there was no point in 'whingeing', he looked for the best deal for Westland's shareholders. A takeover offer from the American helicopter giant, Sikorsky, seemed likely to be the best deal, but he sought better offers elsewhere. Meanwhile he lobbied in Whitehall to make sure that the maximum orders would be forthcoming to make the loss-making company as attractive as possible to any purchaser.

The 'moving of the goal posts' came when Heseltine suddenly arrived on the scene. Cuckney had reason for irritation if only because Heseltine had not shown much interest in Westland's troubles up till then. Now he expressed outrage that the rescue package being put together by Cuckney was going to be expensive for the British taxpayer and was effectively a sell-out to the Americans. The quantity of blood spilt on the political carpet was particularly ironic in view of the official government line – that the whole business was essentially a commercial transaction. As the Prime Minister frequently put it, the decision must be left to the Westland shareholders.

A battle then developed between the American solution (the formula for a sale to Sikorsky, devised by Cuckney and backed by Brittan) and a rival solution, dependent on the formation of a European consortium, which Heseltine tried to encourage with all his formidable enthusiasm. The Prime Minister's interpretation of governmental neutrality was to come down firmly on the 'American' side. Given her prejudices on Europe, not to mention her prejudices about Michael Heseltine, she was not inclined to become any less partisan when it became clear how vigorously he was pushing the European alternative. There was a meeting of minds between her and Cuckney. He seems to have developed a private line to her in the course of the battle, on the not unreasonable ground that when two members of the government were at loggerheads, he was entitled to go over their heads to Downing Street. The old methods of the Establishment were still valid.

The story of the eventual victory of the 'American' over the 'European' solution – after the spectacular resignation of Heseltine, the humiliating resignation of Brittan and the discrediting of the Prime Minister and several of her personal staff – has been told often enough before (see *Heseltine: the unauthorized biography* by Julian Critchley).

It was strictly true that the fate of Westland lay in the hands of its shareholders, and Cuckney's unique qualities as a company chairman were put to the test as opinion among the shareholders swayed, now towards the American, now towards the European option.

As in most cases concerning appeals to the loyalties of shareholders, it is worth remembering the nature of shareholding of the typical British public company. The word 'shareholder' conjures up a picture of little old ladies in Bournemouth. In fact, of course, the people who were deciding the future of Westland were a fairly small number of powerful holders of large blocks of shares – and they were not always the same holders. A remarkable feature of the Westland battle (considering that this was a near-bankrupt company) was the large volume of buying and selling of shares, and a major factor influencing these large shareholders was their assessment of future governmental policy – at the end of the day it was all going to come down to which government would order which helicopters.

Nor could the battle for the shares ignore the purely political tensions in the background. It was because the Prime Minister was so determined in following her interpretation of 'neutrality' that her staff in Downing Street put in train the dubious operation to discredit Heseltine, for which Leon Brittan had to pay the price by resigning. During the fast-moving action, a lot of people in high places did things they no doubt regretted later. John Cuckney was the one person who kept his head, in all senses. It was a virtuoso performance in the Establishment tradition.

Not that he did not have strong personal feelings. Part of

his resentment of Heseltine lay in the way the issue was being presented as a conflict between pro- and anti-Europe lobbies. Cuckney was as much a 'European' as Heseltine – his experience in industry left him in no doubt that salvation for much of British industry meant addressing itself to the Continental market. He had the advantage over the politicians in that he had a clearer picture of the realities of the situation on the ground at Westland. This was a special case of a common plight of British companies in the late twentieth century: a firm with excellent expertise unfortunately not matched by the commercial skills needed in the modern world. That was perhaps the saddest part of the Westland story.

By the end of the Thatcher years, Cuckney was among those industrialists who, looking back, had no doubt that what she had done during the 1980s had been necessary and admirable. He was among a group of business leaders who wrote to *The Times* deploring her departure. A second *Times* letter on the eve of the 1992 election castigated those who were tempted to imagine that a Labour victory might in some way be good for industry. That was when the *Financial Times*, among other worthy institutions, was talking of the need for change. The Cuckneys of this world were at least clear about the dangers of Labour governments.

Perhaps it was as a tribute to his safe hands that the Conservative government later chose him to pursue the Maxwell pensioners' missing millions. Good hunting!

12

First past the post

WOODROW WYATT

A SHREWD journalistic commentator, the not easily impressed Frank Johnson, once called Lord Wyatt of Weeford the 'single most influential person' of the Thatcherite age. That might be pitching it a bit high. But Margaret Thatcher certainly had reason to be grateful to Woodrow Wyatt, a newspaper columnist, tele-pundit and reformed ex-socialist who became a banner waver for Thatcherism.

Not everyone took Woodrow seriously. Some, indeed, would say that two things about him tell it all. One is his choice of floppy bow ties. The other is that when he was at Oxford, in the late Thirties, a group of hearty young gentlemen decided that he should be thrown into the lake at Worcester College. It wasn't his bow ties they objected to, but his penchant for wearing black silk pyjamas. People faced with total immersion for wearing black pyjamas either sink without trace or they survive, to make successive generations of colleagues want to throw them into lakes. Woodrow survived.

The mere length of his career in public life, from the 1950s to the 1990s, makes it impossible to ignore him. He was the great survivor. His politics started with the 'Keep Left' group of the Labour party and ended with zealous Thatcherism. He happily contributed his thoughts to the whole gamut of journalism from *Tribune* to the most capitalist of the capitalist press.

He survived the war, although he narrowly escaped being court-martialled for telling his commanding officer he was no good at his job. He survived the post-war Attlee government, when he first became a Labour MP and served briefly as a junior Defence Minister. He survived electoral defeat (at Grantham, of all constituencies) and successfully switched careers from politics to tele-journalism. As the Labour party evolved, he survived the death of his hero Hugh Gaitskell and the arrival of Harold Wilson. But in a sense the full flowering of his career did not come until he established a rapport with Margaret Thatcher.

It was she, apparently, who made the first approach. On the face of it, it was a surprising alliance. As a journalist Woodrow had been less than complimentary about her: 'She vigorously displays that pernickety bossiness and prissy self-righteousness which is so irritating to male associates,' he wrote in one of his newspaper columns. Nevertheless, Wood-row clearly interested Margaret, at the time when she became leader of the Conservative party in 1975. She consulted that grand old wordsmith and authority on self-righteousness, John Junor, who was among her favourite journalists. 'Ask him to lunch,' Junor advised.

The resultant encounter in the Thatcher home at Flood Street was a meeting of minds. Wyatt describes it in his memoirs, *Confessions of an Optimist*:

> I found her much less scratchy than I remembered, more mature and broader in her mind, and pleasantly appealing with pretty legs and complexion. She won me over. The strength of her determination and the simplicity of her rational ideas uncluttered by intellectual confusion convinced me that she was the first party leader I had met,

apart from Gaitskell, who might check Britain's slide and possibly begin to reverse it.

Woodrow's judgements on the prettiness of Hugh Gaitskell's legs and complexion are not on record, and it might be thought that admiration for Hugh Gaitskell was an unlikely basis for conversion to Thatcherism. But the 1975 Flood Street meeting resulted in the future Prime Minister recruiting a doughty champion to her cause at a time when she needed all the recruits she could get.

Why had a man like Woodrow Wyatt become a socialist in the first place? The short answer seems to be that it was to spite his father, a prep school headmaster who, according to his son in the book just quoted, had many unlikeable characteristics. The senior Wyatt's views on socialists were simple: 'they are traitors and they haven't even got any money'. The young Woodrow told himself that if his father disapproved of such people so strongly there must be some good in socialism.

It was clearly not socialist egalitarianism that attracted him. On the contrary, at Oxford (where he was backed financially not by his father but by an uncle) he enjoyed the good life and rubbing shoulders with the élite. Socialism for him was not a matter of taking vows of poverty; or of chastity. In all this he resembled the Labour men with whom he was to consort – people like Gaitskell, John Strachey and Tony Crosland.

He belonged to a generation that took it for granted that after the war a brave new world was to be ushered in. Woodrow Wyatt, although perhaps a lot more bumptious, was not all that different from other expensively educated young ex-officers who at the end of the Second World War found themselves, often to their surprise, sitting on the Labour benches in the Commons after the 1945 landslide election, supplementing their MP's salary by writing thoughtful articles in the more progressive newspapers about the importance of a sensibly planned society.

Wyatt attracted some notice in the 1945 Parliament, and for the last few months of the Attlee government he was Under-Secretary of State for War. (He got to know Monty – whose signature a few years earlier had determined that Major Wyatt should not be court-martialled but merely transferred to some other theatre of war.)

In the 1955 general election Woodrow's Commons constituency was redistributed and an attempt to find an alternative seat failed when the voters of Grantham resisted his charms. But fate was kind. The then incredibly distinguished American TV personality, Ed Murrow, had selected Grantham, presumably because of its ordinariness, as a suitable base from which to report the British election to the American public. Wyatt as Labour candidate featured in the Murrow programme, which of course was not shown on British TV but happened to be seen by the then head of BBC Current Affairs, Grace Wyndham Goldie. Mrs Goldie recognized a lively talent that sparkled on the small screen, and Woodrow Wyatt was launched on a new career as an interviewer for *Panorama*, about to enter its great period as flagship of the BBC.

These were still the pioneer days of television, and on *Panorama* he contributed to the development of TV journalism by moving away from what had been the deferential BBC style of interviewing. He was no respecter of persons, or institutions. The fact that he was an ex-Labour MP was felt to give an appearance of balance. His best-known achievement on *Panorama* was to expose Communist attempts to take over major trade unions. This did him no harm with his friends on the right wing of the Labour party of the time. But it heightened suspicions about him on the left – and eventually also helped to qualify him to take part in the Thatcherite revolution.

His reports on union skullduggery were excellent reporting

of the exposé type. Arguably it was also a very partial type
of journalism – a point which was to be thrown back at him.
Years later, part of the Wyatt persona was to scourge the
'left-wing media establishment': the poacher turned game-
keeper. One man's bias is another man's frank and fearless
reporting.

Frankness about the unions raised problems when he tried
to make a come-back as a Labour MP, but he succeeded in
1959, and returned to the Opposition side in the Commons
in the heyday of Harold Macmillan's Premiership. Politics
had changed since he had last sat on the green benches. So
had Woodrow Wyatt. Truth to tell, by 1959 he did not fit
easily into the great party of the working class. This was even
more obvious when he took to owning racehorses and (using
his wife's money) became a newspaper proprietor on a small
scale by buying the *Banbury Guardian*. It was a time when a
fashionable term of abuse was 'champagne socialist'. In due
course Woodrow also became a friend of the Queen Mother.

But becoming a capitalist did not mean that he was an
admirer of the Macmillan government. His view of that
government was indeed probably not dissimilar from that
formed retrospectively, a dozen years later, by one of
Harold's junior ministers, Margaret Thatcher. When Woodrow and Margaret become cronies in the 1970s, one thing on
which they were able to agree was that Macmillanite government had been concerned too much with style and too little
with the fact that in the 1960s the country was fast going to
the dogs. However, the Thatcher–Wyatt rapport was yet to
come. In the early Sixties, Woodrow was still a Labour MP,
who had formed the view that the most likely chance of getting rid of Macmillan, and all he stood for, was a Lib-Lab
pact. In Neanderthal Labour circles, this was heresy – tribal
treachery. Labour colleagues reacted rather like those Oxford
hearties of yesteryear.

His judgement on the Lib-Lab idea was wrong, as events
later proved. Macmillanism was not to be destroyed by

117

trendy, enlightened left-of-centre liberalism. Nor indeed was it destroyed by Neanderthal socialism. It eventually sank under assault from a well-aimed handbag, with Woodrow Wyatt cheering on the sidelines.

But if he was wrong about the case for a Lib-Lab pact, he was surely right in his later analysis about how Margaret Thatcher came to move the political goalposts. In *Confessions of an Optimist*, he notes that he himself 'never became a Tory'; he supported Mrs Thatcher 'as the person most likely to lessen the British decline'. And he explains his point of view by telling a story about the Churchill family.

One evening, when staying with Randolph Churchill at East Bergholt, I had a furious row with him. That was not difficult: this one was sparked off by my referring to his father, Winston, as a Tory. Randolph thumped the table, shouting in a rage, 'We were never Tories and never will be. We just make use of the Tory Party.' Quite. Mrs Thatcher is not a Tory either. Nor am I.

Woodrow served Mrs Thatcher, if not the Tory party, faithfully. She had him knighted and then elevated to the House of Lords. In the Upper House he was active in arguing, for instance, for a statutory duty of 'impartiality' to be imposed on broadcasters – a profession which had upset her on various occasions during her Premiership.

He had become one of her familiar spirits. All Prime Ministers feel the need for people, outside the immediate circle of colleagues, who can articulate their own deepest instincts and prejudices and tell them things that colleagues would not, or dare not, tell them. If the familiar spirit can make the Prime Minister laugh, so much the better. By the late 1980s, there seems to have been a lot of bouncing of ideas between Woodrow and Margaret. He had that most important facility of power in Westminster: access to No. 10.

Influence derived from the bouncing of ideas in various

ways. By the late Eighties Woodrow, although 70 years old, was still a vigorous columnist. His words distilled the essence of Thatcherite wisdom drawn from the source itself – on trade unionism, on the failings of journalists and broadcasters, and perhaps above all on the unique leadership qualities of Margaret Thatcher. He had a readership that added up to literally millions and that was drawn from across the whole spectrum, for he wrote for *The Times* as well as for the *News of the World* (both owned, as it happened, by Rupert Murdoch, another man with access to No. 10). The Thatcherite revolution had always been more a revolution of ideas than one of economics or of political tactics. Lord Wyatt kept that revolution in good heart.

The other part of his influence, the extent of which we can only guess at, came from his role as familiar spirit. He probably reinforced, by drawing on his media experience, the Prime Minister's feelings that her policies were always being traduced and distorted by many newspapers and TV programmes. Her suspicion of the 'media establishment' was part of her basic suspicion of the Conservative tradition of trying to find an enlightened middle way. Conservative traditions were anathema to Woodrow Wyatt too – perhaps because he was still reacting against his father. The irony of his rapport with Mrs Thatcher, some might say, was that he himself was almost a parody of an Establishment figure.

13

Men of the Cloth
IMMANUEL JAKOBOVITS
and
EDWARD NORMAN

MARGARET ROBERTS was brought up as a Methodist, and married in Wesley's chapel in City Road. She evolved into an Anglican while progressing upwards in the Tory party, but by that time the Anglican Church had evolved too. It was no longer the Tory party at prayer. Sometimes, indeed, during the Thatcher administration, the Prime Minister wondered if the Archbishop of Canterbury had ambitions to be Leader of the Opposition.

For spiritual comfort, the Prime Minister looked elsewhere. The theology of two men particularly attracted her, and neither of them was in the conventional Anglican mould. One was a brilliant *enfant terrible* on the radical Right of the Anglican clergy, Dr Edward Norman. The other was the Chief Rabbi.

There were considerable similarities between Mrs Thatcher and Immanuel Jakobovits, Chief Rabbi of the United Hebrew Congregations of the British Commonwealth from 1967 to 1990. He shared with her a high degree of self-confidence about what is right and what is wrong. Both had a staunch faith in what they saw as the virtues of the British character.

Britain had been a refuge for the Jakobovits family when they fled the Nazis just before the war. (The Chief Rabbi never forgot what Germany had done, and in his last months in office, when the two Germanies were heading for reunion, he was among those who expressed misgivings. So, too, did Mrs Thatcher.)

Jakobovits was an orthodox and traditionalist rabbi, but with a difference. When he had a spell at the new Fifth Avenue Synagogue in New York, he saw his role as trying to 'make orthodoxy elegant and fashionable and to show that you don't have to live in squalor to be a strictly traditional Jew'.

When he came to London as Chief Rabbi in 1967, it was not, on the face of it, a particularly good time for either orthodoxy or conservatism. There was something almost unreal, in the Swinging Sixties, about a rabbi telling his people that on the Sabbath they shouldn't drive their cars or even switch on the electric light. Nevertheless, even in the Sixties there was an important, if minority, market for conservatism among people of all faiths, or none. By the 1970s Jakobovits was becoming well known outside his own faith for his advocacy of traditional moral values: he believed in marital fidelity; he condemned homosexuality; he stood for the traditional Jewish pride in supporting oneself and one's family, and not relying on the State for welfare.

He was expressing robust views that struck a chord in many Gentile hearts. Conservatives (with a small c) were extremely uneasy about the Britain they saw when they looked around them in the 1970s. It was not just the sexual excesses of the Sixties. Look at all the spongers on the Welfare State, they said. Look at the work-shy trade unions. Look at the government of Harold Wilson – not much reassurance there about the moral fibre of the nation.

Moreover, an increasing number of Conservatives, with a capital C, were beginning to suffer from an uneasy conscience about the Harold Macmillan kind of Toryism. Purists might point out that Macmillan had not actually said that all is well with a nation which has 'never had it so good', but the time was ripe for a whiff of puritanism. With the benefit of hindsight, we now know that in the 1970s, political revolution was on the way. No bigger than a man's hand, Thatcherism was beginning to appear on the horizon.

Revolutions need prophets, and the prophets of Thatcherism were not to be found in the mainstream of either Church or State. In the field of political theory the pacemakers emerged from what had been regarded as the extreme, sometimes loony right-wing fringes of the Tory party. Some of the most successful prophets of the New Right were erstwhile left-wing polemicists like Paul Johnson, Woodrow Wyatt and Alfred Sherman, who veered sharply across the political spectrum. They were astute enough to see that in the 1970s it was going to be the New Right, not the old Left, who could play the anti-Establishment card. No wonder the Church of England was confused. It found itself tarred by the new (Tory) revolutionaries as part of an effete, ineffective form of woolly liberal do-goodery that had to be swept away.

Against this background, the Chief Rabbi, who was an articulate and intelligent figure, took on a significance that he might not otherwise have enjoyed. Already he had attracted admiring glances from moral conservatives for speaking out clearly at a time when many of the Anglican clergy were inclined to fudge the issue of what was right and what was wrong. Now he started to interest the new political Conservatives. His views on the family, and on the superiority of private rather than State charity, fitted in well with the demands from the radical New Right for a rethink of Britain's Welfare State. One of their rallying calls was that the State should leave people's money in their own pockets and let them make their own arrangements for providing their own pensions, their own health care and for the education of their own children. That was no more than Jews had said for centuries.

(One of Jakobovits's biggest achievements as Chief Rabbi was to increase the number of Jewish schools in England.)

Conservatives were changing their ethos as well as their policies. The party has always been a coalition in continual debate, but it was now shifting to incorporate new constituencies which had formerly not felt at home in the Conservative party. British Jewry was one such constituency. British Jews had always tended to be suspicious of the Tory Establishment, and the feeling was reciprocated. Even if you were an outstandingly successful entrepreneur – perhaps *particularly* if you were a successful entrepreneur – you were not necessarily welcome in High Tory places. Small wonder that middle-class Jews, if they were politically minded, had gravitated towards the Labour party. But the new Thatcherite party – with its emphasis on the virtues of pulling oneself up by one's bootstraps, and its rejection of the old 'gentlemanly' prejudice that making money is something nice people do but do not talk about – was a different animal altogether.

The attractions of the new party for Jews were not diminished by the fact that Mrs Thatcher's great guru of the Seventies was Sir Keith Joseph. When Keith Joseph first entered Parliament, he had been one of only two Jewish Tory MPs; by the time Mrs Thatcher had established herself as Prime Minister, he was only one of a substantial number of Jews in influential positions in her Cabinet. The change may not have been a conscious strategy, but it was significant. A Jewish Tory MP was said to have exclaimed of Francis Pym, 'One of us, he is not . . .'

Keith Joseph's Centre for Policy Studies was not just a think-tank evolving a new intellectual basis for Tory policy. It provided a focus for attracting influential people who would not have fitted in to the old Establishment. The most notable was Lord Young, but he was only one of many, and only one of the Jewish businessmen to be recruited. By the time Margaret Thatcher became Prime Minister in 1979 she had an array of talent stacked up behind her, drawn from sources that had not been available to Tory leaders in the past.

While this was happening, the New Right girded its loins intellectually and spiritually. In 1978 it received spiritual succour from an unlikely direction: from the BBC's Reith Lectures.

The lecturer, the Revd Edward Norman, was a 40-year-old bachelor history don, Dean of Peterhouse, Cambridge. He was an ordained Anglican priest (and by all accounts a dedicated pastoral worker), but he was about as far as could be imagined from the image of the cosy C of E parson of folklore. He was a brilliant scholar. He was frighteningly well read in some branches of politics. As a teacher he had a reputation for acerbic wit. His instinct was to stir things up, not to look for happy compromises. (This was one facet of his character that appealed to Mrs T.) He did not suffer fools gladly. He was not disposed to defer automatically to the great men of the Church. And he loved the kind of arguments which end up by showing that intellectually the emperor (or the bishop) has no clothes.

His Reith Lectures, delivered as the Tories were finalizing the platform on which they were to stand in the 1979 election, were concerned with theology, not politics, but there was a clear parallel with the Thatcherite revolution in political thinking. He roundly condemned churchmen for over-emphasis on social idealism. Effectively he was rebutting the belief that the woolly ideals of the Wilson–Callaghan Labour party had some kind of moral superiority. More significantly, it was also an attack on the 'wet' variety of Conservatism.

For Edward Norman was no paid-up Tory. His background was certainly not that of a traditional Tory leader. His father had been a stockbroker's clerk. He had no natural sympathy for the relaxed philosophy of the public schoolboys he encountered when they reached Cambridge. It was often pointed out that he had himself once attended the same grammar school (Chatham House School, Ramsgate) that produced Edward Heath.

Politically he was fundamentally an anti-Establishment man. He was accused of wanting to 'privatize the Church of England'. It fitted into a pattern of belief that the ruling classes of England had done little to allow ordinary people to work out their own destiny. He claimed to have been a member of the Labour party as a sixth-former. As a young don in the Sixties he was inclined to be in sympathy with the radical student movement. Perhaps because it takes a radical to know a radical, he could be scathing about armchair revolutionaries who sympathized with left-wing South American dictatorships. He was quick to point to cases where the Church got itself trapped into doing the Marxists' work for them.

Like Mrs Thatcher, he interpreted the gospel of loving one's neighbour in a way which was not a recipe for social democracy. One story of his influence in high places told of a meeting during the Thatcher regime of the Conservative Philosophy Group, attended by her, by Norman and by Enoch Powell. Conversation became heated, and at one point the Prime Ministerial voice was heard clearly announcing: 'Dr Norman, you are a prophet.'

Even if he did no more than provide Downing Street with another lodestar for taking philosophical cross-bearings, Edward Norman had an important influence on political development in the 1980s. But, like Jakobovits, he also provided something else the Thatcherites needed: a scholarly, clerical mind that would give both intellectual and theological respectability to their prejudices.

As the unemployment figures rose and inner city rioting upset liberal consciences, the government of the early 1980s found itself under fire from clerics of all denominations. Bishops became political commentators. The cricketing Bishop of Liverpool, David Sheppard, was much quoted in the media on the social problems of underprivileged Merseyside. The confrontation between Anglicanism and Thatcherism reached a peak with the publication of a document called 'Faith in the Cities'. Its social message offended a significant number of Anglican parsons, because Edward Norman was not alone in seeing a moral basis for Thatcherism. But the most robust critique of 'Faith in the Cities' came from Chief Rabbi Jakobovits, who published a counterblast, 'From Doom to Hope'.

A Chief Rabbi was in a powerful position to take part in a debate which centred largely on how society should treat its racial minorities, in this case the inner city blacks who had rioted in Brixton and elsewhere. Jakobovits's 'From Doom to Hope' pointed to the experience of Jews over the centuries arriving in host countries as an oppressed minority, but successfully lifting themselves up by their own efforts, by educating themselves, by caring for their own people. It was the same message, delivered in a very different tone of voice, that came from Norman Tebbit when he told the disaffected young to 'get on their bikes'. Official approval came for the Chief Rabbi. In 1981 he had been knighted. Now he became a life peer. The Establishment was indeed taking on a Thatcherite gloss.

In a decade, Margaret Thatcher changed British society, and shifted many of the national goalposts. Not least, she changed the range of people who set standards for the rest of us. 'The Establishment' may have been an overworked phrase and a misleading concept, but there it was. A certain kind of public-school ethos, a certain kind of comfortable text from the pulpit, a certain kind of reassuring message from platforms shared by captains of industry on the one hand and trade union leaders on the other – all this was once part of the British way of life. It seemed simplistic to the Jakobovitses and the Edward Normans. In any event, it has gone. Is that a good thing?

14

The Selling of the Prime Minister
BERNARD INGHAM

THE PALACE of Westminster is full of strange traditions which carry their own logic. Nobody is allowed to die in the Palace. Anyone so presumptuous as to challenge this rule is bundled into an ambulance and deemed to be dead on arrival at Westminster Hospital. Death does not exist in the Palace. By the same token, one of the more remote of the neo-Gothic towers contains a room which officially does not exist, rather like the secret room in a Victorian novel which accommodates the mad bastard cousin the family never talk about.

High up near Big Ben is the room where the lobby journalists assemble regularly to be briefed about government policy. But these meetings officially never happen. The terms in which briefings are 'not conducted' must not be quoted. It is part of the rich tapestry of Westminster that visiting professors of political practice from American Mid-Western colleges find charming.

The convention that British governments feed journalists with news on a non-attributable basis has been formally in existence for more than half a century, and informally goes back longer than that. It is a cosy, gentlemanly, slightly hypocritical arrangement that some would say is typical of the way the country was run when it was in the hands of the Establishment. As such, lobby briefings seemed ripe for the chop when the Thatcherite revolution against the Establishment took place in 1979. Not so. The lobby system prospered to become a vital weapon in Margaret Thatcher's armoury during the political battles of the 1980s. Which brings us to the character of the Prime Minister's press secretary for the whole of that long decade, Bernard Ingham.

Much has been written of Bernard Ingham, and even more spoken in the course of Westminster conversation, often in heated tones. But one of the points made most frequently about him – that he was an improbable choice for the No. 10 job – can be disposed of quickly, though it is true that he once stood as a Labour candidate in a local government election, and as a journalist he was once on the staff of the *Guardian*.

Bernard Ingham came of solid Labour, Nonconformist stock. The Ingham home was in Hebden Bridge in the Upper Calder Valley in the Pennines, which seems to have been the Yorkshire equivalent of one of those Welsh valleys peopled by the salt of the earth. The young Inghams were well fed – but nothing fancy. The height of luxury was dock pudding, a fried concoction of dock leaves, nettles, onions and oatmeal.

The atmosphere, one suspects, was not entirely unlike that in the Roberts family further south in Grantham. There was a lot of chapel-going. There was an awe of education. Bernard failed the 11-plus, so his parents scrimped for him to go to grammar school. There was, though, a lively Yorkshire interest in sport, which always put a gloss on Bernard's interpretation of political events. When the famous letter appeared in *The Times* in which 364 economists predicted that Mrs Thatcher's economic policies would lead to disaster, he said he could always remember the exact number: it was the same as Len Hutton's record-breaking Test score against the Australians at the Oval in 1938. Bernard was brought up on the

Daily Herald. So he had at least the right political instincts for the *Guardian*. His solid reporting skills, learned the hard way on the *Hebden Bridge Times*, apparently impressed the *Guardian*'s then editor, Alastair Hetherington, although their first meeting was scarcely a meeting of minds: afterwards a rather baffled Ingham said the only subject he could remember discussing was the importance of the beaver in preserving the aquatic environment of North America. But Hetherington offered him the job, and did not object to his continuing to contribute to Yorkshire politics by writing an anonymous, rumbustious Tory-baiting column in the local Labour party paper. But anyone who thinks that such peculiarities prevented a man from becoming an *apparatchik* of the Thatcherite revolution does not understand what Thatcherism is all about. Bernard's appointment, only a few months after Margaret herself arrived in Downing Street, may have been to some extent fortuitous – he was recommended to her simply as the best operator in the team of Whitehall information officers – but it proved to be one of the most effective she ever made. He became far more than an *apparatchik*. By the late 1980s, still a civil servant, and still several grades down from the top of the Whitehall pecking order, he was being talked of, not entirely flippantly, as a Deputy Prime Minister.

He was not, of course, the only one-time Labour supporter to emerge as a favoured member of the Thatcher entourage, but he proved more durable than some others. The Ingham story is indeed a reminder that many Thatcherites were people who used to fit naturally into the Labour party. Their politics were based on the gut feeling that for far too long the British decision-making process had been in the hands of an effete, spoiled, silver-tongued, privileged minority out of touch with most men in the street. 'One of the things you and I have in common, Bernard,' Mrs Thatcher is once said to have remarked to him, 'is that neither of us is a *smooth* person.'

Bernard Ingham was a Yorkshireman of what is usually called the bluff kind. (Another misconception about Thatcherism is that it was an imposition of Home Counties values on an unwilling North.) When Ingham denounced the enemies of his political mistress it was in tones reminiscent of his fellow Yorkshireman J. B. Priestley broadcasting during the war about the iniquities of Adolf Hitler – how could honest English folk be taken in by such villainy? Righteous indignation was a hallmark of Thatcherite politics in the '80s.

On the *Guardian*, he was deputy to the labour editor, Peter Jenkins. Whether he had ambitions to climb up the hierarchy of that newspaper is not clear, but, in the words of Jenkins, 'there was a feeling, probably quite unfounded, that he was not sufficiently metropolitan . . . He was typecast as the provincial journalist down from the sticks.' That was the kind of remark that explained why Ingham sometimes got shirty with the more precious of the journalists he had to deal with on behalf of the Prime Minister. His own view of himself was that he fitted rather well into London life. While on the *Guardian* he began to find his way around the metropolitan watering holes and he has recalled how his regular haunts were the Au Savarin in Charlotte Street and the Old Budapest in Greek Street.

As Chief Press Secretary he was not averse to being entertained by lobby correspondents in the course of duty – unless they had committed some offence against the proprieties of reporting affairs in No. 10. He was a strict disciplinarian and he had a long memory. But on the expense accounts of those who were in good odour he recalled having 'chomped his way through at least a thousand meals' in the cause of serving Margaret: for choice, at Beoty's in St Martin's Lane or the Howard Hotel.

However, it was not directly from the *Guardian* that he reached the Downing Street job. He quit Fleet Street to join the Government Information Service, where he proved himself an efficient, respected and enormously hard-working civil servant. Like all departmental information officers, he found himself on reasonably close terms with ministers – at that time largely Labour. Many ministers find it more congenial to talk over their strategy with their information officers than with their main-line civil servants or their party colleagues.

All government press officers, being civil servants, have a duty not to make themselves purveyors of party propaganda, and there is evidence that at No. 10 Ingham honourably chided his opposite numbers in the Whitehall departments if they were tempted into breaching that rule. How then did he acquire his reputation as a pillar of Thatcherism?

It has always been accepted that the Downing Street press secretary has a co-ordinating role which means that he can legitimately manage news from the various departments to the advantage of the government of the day. Suppose the Treasury warns him that there are disastrous balance-of-payments figures in the pipeline. It may be that the unemployment figures this month are rather good. Very well, it is possible to fix the timing so that both news items are released on the same day, and use the non-attributable briefings to persuade the media that the good news more than balances out the bad. The total thrust of government is shown to good advantage. This sort of thing has been going on under governments of all complexions since the war.

But under Ingham the emphasis may be said to have changed – from the thrust of government to the thrust of the Prime Minister. His loyalty to her developed into an unprecedented partnership between two people who found they had closely compatible ideas on what the Whitehall battles of the 1980s were all about. Margaret, notoriously, liked having people around her who were able to bring her 'solutions, not problems'. Her Cabinet colleagues, even those who were convinced Thatcherites, could fail to present things in the clear black-and-white terms she found natural. Bernard thought in black-and-white terms too. As Mrs Thatcher winged her way round the world to summit meetings, the world press were given robust accounts (off the record) of how, behind closed doors, she had stood up staunchly for British interests in the face of the greed of French farmers or the duplicity of Argentinian dictators.

When Ronald Reagan, nearing the end of his Presidency, visited London briefly in 1988, the headlines next morning showed a remarkable degree of unanimity about the theme of the private working dinner he attended at No. 10. 'Reagan passes Thatcher the torch of peace,' ran the headline of the *Daily Express*. 'He asked her', said the *Daily Mail*, 'to be ready to pick up the torch of freedom and a safer world.'

How did they know what had passed between President and Prime Minister? Non-attributable briefing brings an air of authority – it would not sound so dramatic if reporters had to say: 'The Prime Minister's press secretary claimed that Mrs Thatcher was passed the torch . . .'

An important duty of the No. 10 press secretary has always been to disseminate – in some people's view to leak – an edited version of confidential discussions. Nobody has ever been very clear how this fits in with the rigorous restrictions of the Official Secrets Act on publishing what goes on behind the scenes in Whitehall. Obviously the information circulated will be selective. To put it bluntly, a powerful Prime Minister with a powerful press secretary has little difficulty in putting a gloss on Cabinet decisions.

As two unsmooth people, Margaret and Bernard seem to have found that they were talking the same language. One suspects that they quickly developed a technique for communicating between each other in shorthand: a word, or even a gesture, when they met and the press secretary knew what message he was expected to spell out. And during the 1980s Ingham had probably at least as much day-to-day access to the Prime Minister as any Cabinet member or senior civil servant.

If it was combative phrases the press wanted, Ingham was able to supply them in his own inimitable style. He had a robust sense of humour. When the civil servant Clive Ponting was charged with leaking secrets, he remarked, off the record of course, that he hoped Judge Jeffreys would be presiding. He had his own views on the train of events which led to Michael Heseltine challenging Margaret for the leadership. The train of events started with Michael writing a letter to his constituency chairman, before he was due to set off on a Middle East visit. He had 'lit the blue paper', said Bernard, 'and then retired to a safe distance – in his case to Amman.'

There was scope, obviously, for misunderstanding along the classic lines which got Henry II into trouble when he sounded off in the hearing of courtiers, and his knights rushed off to murder Becket. Henry repented. There is little evidence that Mrs Thatcher ever repented when Bernard galloped off to get rid of troublesome priests.

The best-known example concerned John Biffen, once one of the Cabinet's most astute and dedicated Thatcherites, who then had Doubts. He was Lord Privy Seal and Leader of the House of Commons, a not unimportant post, it might be thought, when Ingham, in an off-the-record briefing, mentioned that he was 'a semi-detached member of the Cabinet'. It was some time before Mrs Thatcher got around to sacking Biffen, but this use of the lobby system opened up a whole new dimension of Prime Ministerial power over her colleagues.

The same technique to undercut the authority of a colleague was employed against Francis Pym, who made a speech, when still a Cabinet member, pointing out various economic difficulties. He found himself compared, off the record, to the wartime radio character Mona Lot. The words (which by convention had never been officially uttered) were Bernard's. The irritation being expressed had its source elsewhere. And in due course Pym lost his job as well as his leader's respect.

When he came to write his memoirs, *Kill the Messenger*, Ingham apologized for both these episodes, defending himself by describing how he was under pressure from journalists to say *something*. He does not seem to have regretted a presumably unauthorized remark he made when the end was near for Margaret and he was asked who, now that Geoffrey Howe had resigned, would be most likely to succeed if Margaret was knocked down by a bus. He started his answer with the old joke that the bus wouldn't dare. Then he decided to name a name: Douglas Hurd. When the inevitable stories appeared he records that he was 'more concerned for Douglas Hurd than for myself'.

The press secretary's job is to express what he knows of the Prime Minister's views. Inevitably he also has input into those views. Apart from anything else, it was through Bernard that Margaret knew what the media were saying. He had input into speeches and answers to parliamentary questions. A Kitchen Cabinet can be more influential than the real thing.

All Prime Ministers need to have familiar spirits around them – people they feel safe with. Basically, this means people who are at home at the top but are not in the running for the Prime Minister's own job – a wholly sympathetic figure that they can bounce ideas off. Sometimes, but only very rarely, the role can be filled by a member of the Cabinet. In the earliest days some of these duties were performed by the 200 per cent loyal Keith Joseph, then some by the equally loyal Willie Whitelaw. Both were gone by the late 1980s and a gap was created which Ingham to some extent filled. He helped to refine the Prime Minister's views and knew how to anticipate them. He had many of the same instincts. Describing his attitude to the sight of Euro-politics in Brussels he would say it reminded him of his old woodwork master at Hebden Bridge Grammar School who, seeing a group of boys talking together at a bench, would approach them, 'block of lignum vitae in hand', and say menacingly, 'Where two or three are gathered, I smell trouble.'

Like the Prime Minister, he was not afraid of the strength

of his own feelings. After the Brighton bombing he visited the injured and bereaved John Wakeham in hospital and recalled being 'so angry that I was not fit to drive myself back home'.

So far as her relations with the media were concerned, Margaret Thatcher's feelings tended to be not so much angry as non-existent. Quite simply, she was not a newspaper reader, except, according to Bernard, that she would glance at the front page of the *Evening Standard*. She would also glance at the Press Association club tape (which had been installed in Downing Street by Clem Attlee, when it was explained to him that he would get the cricket results that way). Margaret Thatcher got her knowledge of what the press were saying about the government from the daily press sum-mary which Bernard personally spent several hours drawing up for her early every morning.

But if there was a degree of detachment from the press, it did not apply to the one radio programme that loomed large in her life. A wartime child, Margaret inevitably expected much of BBC radio. It was natural for her to start the day, while cooking breakfast for Denis, by switching on Radio 4. By the middle of her Premiership her relationship with the *Today* programme was like that of a sensitive child with a horror comic – knowing that it is going to give her bad dreams but too fascinated to lay it down. How much government policy was influenced by Margaret's reaction to something she had heard on *Today*? Certainly, if ministers agreed to take part in the programme, they knew their every word was being listened to avidly.

Bernard Ingham reflected her interest in the *Today* pro-gramme and had an added personal emotional involvement. He records bleakly in *Kill the Messenger* that 'most damage to Government–BBC relations was done between 6.30 and 9 a.m. by my former *Guardian* colleague Brian Redhead'. It was partly the old tension between 'metropolitan' journalism and the austere standards of the *Hebden Bridge Times*. There

137

was a yearning in Bernard, as there was in Margaret, for a return to the simple old virtues of their childhood. He detested it when he saw newspapermen going beyond the simple job of the reporter and editorializing. What he did not seem to realize was that his own role as a press secretary was rather more than simple reporting.

A press secretary is backed by the complex structure of the Whitehall information machine. It was the techniques within that machine that nearly brought disaster for the Thatcher regime during the Westland crisis.

The Westland affair was a unique sequence of events involving complex interdepartmental politicking and at least three ambitious, strong-minded politicians: the Prime Minister herself, the Defence Secretary Michael Heseltine and the Industry Secretary Leon Brittan. At one point in the politicking it was felt that things could be moved nearer a conclusion if the Solicitor-General were to write a letter to Michael Heseltine criticizing the legal basis of something he had done. In the fraught atmosphere of the time, it was apparently decided that the letter, by itself, was not enough: the public relations potential should be exploited; the critical part of the letter should be leaked to the press in order to damage the Heseltine case.

By Whitehall convention, this was a much more serious matter than the leaking of events at Cabinet. Special privileges attach to advice addressed to ministers by law officers. That certainly was the view of the Solicitor-General, who was furious when he saw his words headlined across the newspapers.

Who was responsible? There was never much question about who actually passed quotations from the latter on to the Press Association. This was Colette Bowe, information officer at the Industry Department. It was also clear that she was unhappy about doing so and was under the impression that she was under orders. From whom? This we never knew for certain. MPs investigating the sanguinary aftermath of the leak found that questions relating to the Civil Service's role would be evaded personally by that most notoriously discreet of civil servants, the then Cabinet Secretary, Sir Robert Armstrong. We do know who was eventually made to pay the political price of indiscretion: Miss Bowe's ministerial boss, Leon Brittan, who was persuaded to resign. But he was clearly only one party to a PR coup that went wrong.

The 1980s, it has been said, were the decade when public relations came of age. This was inevitable in the age which rediscovered the market economy. When all things have to be measured by the market, the public are exposed to powerful persuasion to buy what is offered to them.

At one time, Conservatives would have argued that public relations and the 'organization of information' were part of the froth of socialism, not the sort of thing that hard-headed pragmatic statesmen ought to get themselves involved in. This was not true of the Conservative government that came to office in 1979. In the second half of the 1980s, the sums spent by government on advertising quadrupled, from £22 million to £86 million a year. The privatization strategy depended for its success on persuasion – on 'telling Sid' the merits of buying shares in the once-nationalized industries. Reorganization of the Health Service was sold on a huge scale, using all the hype of a commercial 'new product launch'. The Department of Trade and Industry's 'Enterprise Initiative' was a massive exercise in persuasion. Meanwhile, at general elections, promotional skills were refined to ever more sophisticated levels. And Bernard Ingham, the local paper reporter from Hebden Bridge whose ambition was once to be a Labour councillor in Leeds, was at the heart of the presentational revolution.

15

With rod and gun in the Falklands
MAX HASTINGS

THE FALKLANDS War marked the turning point of the Thatcher years. Before the war in 1982, the Prime Minister was seen by many who had voted for her as a grim necessity – she may have been doing the right thing, but as a person she did not attract. After the Falklands, they liked her.

The Falklands War helped round her as a character because it did not fit into the pattern of what her government had been doing up until then. It was certainly not a monetarist war. Indeed, a number of the strongest monetarists in her entourage were among those who questioned whether it made sense to face the appalling risks involved, and to commit the material and moral resources needed, in retaking the Falklands. It was a war which seemed to belong to an age long before Thatcherism. It was a campaign that Kipling, or the *Boy's Own Paper*, might have invented for readers of gripping yarns. But it was no fiction. It represented something that was real and fundamental to most British people. The determination with which it was fought reached parts of the national consciousness that the economics of Thatcherism could never reach. From that moment, Thatcherism meant much more than monetarism. It was also the kind of war that people had thought could never happen again – derring-do in a faraway corner of the globe, in defence of a beleaguered little band of fellow-Britons. The task-force sailed with the crowds cheering and the bands playing and it ended with men in khaki camouflage marching triumphantly into Port Stanley.

The difference from the colourful imperial campaigns of Victorian times – leaving aside that it was fought with weapons that were horrifyingly modern – was that the British at home were able, thanks to today's communication techniques, to follow the campaign hour by hour, and they did so with ever-increasing admiration. The profession of war correspondent took on a new lease of life, and the outstanding correspondent proved to be Max Macdonald Hastings. To repeat a phrase that had been much used back in 1945, he had 'a good war'.

As it happened, 1945 was the year in which Max Hastings was born. He had an impressive journalistic parentage. His father, Macdonald Hastings, was himself a war correspondent and a literary gent with shootin' and fishin' overtones. His mother, Anne Scott-James, was a very different kind of journalist, a pioneer of the personalized style of newspaper writing that was to become the norm in the upmarket Sunday papers of the Swinging Sixties. The Hastings–Scott-James marriage, while it was one of talents, was eventually not a successful one: after a divorce, Anne Scott-James went on to marry the brilliant cartoonist and observer of British society's mores, Osbert Lancaster.

The young Hastings grew up in an atmosphere of talent and style, but without the benefit of some of the more homely background a child needs. He lived, and went on living, in a world which always seemed rather larger than life. This certainly applied to his physique. At six foot five inches, Max Hastings was a difficult man to ignore.

He burst on the Fleet Street scene in the mid-Sixties like a character out of John Buchan: a man of action in search of adventure, but with undoubted intellectual gifts. He had been an exhibitioner at his Oxford college, which in fact he left early because he was in a hurry to get to the top.

In journalism he established himself not only as a versatile reporter but also as an impressive author of books on military history: *Bomber Command* (which won a Somerset Maugham Prize); *Montrose: the King's Champion*; *Das Reich*; and *Overlord* – hundreds of thousands of words rolled off his typewriter, and they were well-chosen words. He could claim that his books represented serious research as well as reading matter that people bought in airport lounges.

It is impossible not to see a deliberate streak of defiance in his choice of subject matter. This after all was the time when the fashionable way to make a name in journalism was in almost anything other than military matters – the arts, or economics, or social compassion. Politics were dominated by Harold Wilson and Edward Heath, and the serious papers were full of articles about National Plans, or the white heat of technology, or Getting Into Europe, or Whither the Liberal Party? Meanwhile Hastings, as a war correspondent, was finding exciting stories in the Middle East, in Angola, in Indochina and in Ulster.

At a time when newspapers were talking about brave new worlds, Hastings was wilfully traditional, and delighted in teasing, in his loud self-confident voice, the Sixties idealists and the purveyors of radical chic. He built up a whole persona of the bluff, man-of-action reactionary: his dogs (and of course dogs were essential in the John Buchan world) were given names like Tweedie (after Jill Tweedie, the fashionable radical writer of the time) and Stokely (Stokely Charmichael, the black activist).

Meanwhile – for he was enormously prolific – he became one of the relatively tiny band of writers or journalists who make real money. He was able to set himself up in a house of some size in Northamptonshire, where his wife could ride to hounds and he could shoot. It was not always clear which

143

he enjoyed more – the reality of squiredom, or the fact that his attitudes outraged people he felt deserved to be outraged.

There was a fetching touch of self-parody about him. When, in 1986, he became Editor of the *Daily Telegraph*, he decided that the décor of the Editor's room overlooking Fleet Street ought to be different from what it had been under his predecessor, Bill Deedes. Deedes had made a positive virtue of not caring about the material conditions in which he worked ('I put up with much worse in the war, dear boy'). Hastings replaced Deedes's battered old typewriter with a word processor and ostentatiously kept his mobile telephone on view. Stuffed birds appeared around the room, on the grounds that since he was always being criticized for shooting things, he might as well show off what he shot. But there was probably no conscious self-parody in the appearance on the wall of a painting of his wife in the role of lady of the manor.

Hastings got the job as Editor of the *Telegraph* entirely on the basis of his experience as a reporter and writer. He had no experience of the mysteries of Fleet Street editorial management processes. Some might say that was a positive advantage.

His reporting throughout the Sixties and Seventies had earned him considerable respect in Fleet Street, if not always affection among colleagues. He was never one of the boys. On assignments he was not known for hunting with the pack. He was not a team man. His liking for tough missions did not mean that he believed in roughing it – there was a legend that as a war correspondent he would arrive on the battlefield with a Fortnums hamper. His expense accounts featured in folklore. There is a tale, possibly apocryphal, about him being dispatched to the aftermath of the Birmingham bombings and arriving in a taxi – nothing unusual in that, except that it was a London taxi, hailed in Fleet Street and commandeered for the duration.

He was hard to classify. He was neither the trendy kind of journalist nor one of the more typical grey, conscientious hacks who actually do most of the work on newspapers. He was certainly not a conviction journalist, of the type who was beginning to emerge during the 1970s, preaching monetarism and Thatcherism before Thatcher. Politically Hastings liked to describe himself as a journalist who happened to be a Conservative. He gave the impression that it was a slightly improper question – it was like asking a well brought-up young man about religion when everybody knows that all decent chaps are C of E.

When the Thatcher years began, in 1979, Max Hastings was thus a good example of the Thatcherite virtues of sturdy independence and of the incentive value of material rewards. In his lifestyle, and general outlook, he was closer to the old kind of Conservative who believed his politics were a matter of style and instinct rather than of political and economic theory. This was the Max Hastings who set off for the Falklands in the spring of 1982. He was one of a very mixed bag of journalists. Just as the task-force had been put together in a hurry, so had the press corps sent to accompany it. Often it had been a question of who happened to be available on the day when the Ministry of Defence announced that places were available. And the press were probably no more prescient than anyone else about the magnitude of what was about to happen. There was nothing casual, however, about Hastings's sense of mission. He recalled, later, 'standing in the kitchen in Northamptonshire and saying to my wife, "I feel it's for this moment that I was born".'

His advantage over his rivals in the press corps lay not only in his immense store of military knowledge, or his physique, which made him fitter than the average reporter when it came to yomping across the island moorland. He had a rapport with the top brass. They recognized that the message he was seeking to send back to the UK was precisely what they themselves would like to articulate. The censorship rules may not have been twisted to suit him, but there were ways of making choppers available to allow Hastings to be in the right place

145

at the right time. Communication with the UK was of course in the hands of the Services, and one dispatch could be given priority over others. A pooling arrangement which had been agreed meant that the Hastings dispatches appeared in a range of newspapers.

Hastings's personality did not incline him to ponder over-much about whether he was being a good team player by press corps standards. His own robust summing-up was: 'You are playing to win. You are not playing to play the game.'

The spectacular climax to the individualistic Hastings approach came with the taking of Port Stanley. He strode in ahead of most of the troops. It was not an episode calculated to endear him to colleagues; nor was it calculated to diminish his own assessment of himself. The long-standing effect of the Falklands on Hastings – as indeed in the case of the Prime Minister – is probably to be seen in terms of self-confidence, and of fulfilling a destiny.

It is not clear when he saw the *Daily Telegraph* as something to be liberated, as he had helped to liberate Port Stanley; he had never had ambitions to become a newspaper administrator. But he certainly had strong views about the *Telegraph*. Over the years, it had come to offend him deeply, not for what it was or what it did but because of what it failed to do. Here was the paper that could have been the vehicle for precisely the kind of writing that he believed in, with precisely the potential readership that would appreciate the sentiments which were his, but which was manifestly failing to seize its opportunities. The standards of reporting were largely uninspired. The whole presentation seemed unprofessional. There was, if you like, a Thatcherite streak in his irritation. He arrived at the *Telegraph* with the same kind of suspicion of its traditions that Mrs Thatcher, arriving in Downing Street, had of the Whitehall establishment, and indeed of the whole British establishment which had allowed the country to get into such a mess.

The problems of the *Daily Telegraph* group in the mid-

Eighties were in a sense the problems of the UK economy writ large. The print unions had not only been sucking the paper's lifeblood but had also imposed restrictions that inhibited effective action throughout the whole business operation. This scandalous situation applied to other newspapers too. One difference with the *Telegraph* was that it was owned by a company running nothing but newspapers which was therefore unable to fall back on profits from elsewhere. Perhaps even more important, it lacked the cross-fertilization of management ideas which would have come from other parts of a widely based group – ideas which might have saved it from disastrous commercial policies. The further fact that it was a family business, run up until 1985 by Lord Hartwell on paternalistic lines, did not make it any easier to avert the tragedy which befell it that year. Hopelessly overborrowed, the company had to be sold, to the Canadian entrepreneur Conrad Black, who brought in a new chief executive (Andrew Knight) and a new editor in the shape of Hastings.

The new regime arrived, like Mrs Thatcher in Downing Street in 1979, with all the fervour of revolutionaries. This involved not only a faith in change, sometimes change apparently for change's sake, but also a driving conviction, as with revolutionaries down the ages, that wisdom starts here – that nothing was right in the past. Hastings did not help himself by being unwilling to consult staff he had inherited, although he professed to be aware of his lack of experience. 'The only experience I've had of managing staff', he would say, apparently in all seriousness, 'is of hiring and firing my gardeners.' One likes to imagine that, overall, gardeners are handled with more respect than *Telegraph* journalists received at the time.

The justification for the ferocity of the Hastings methods was the customary argument in cases of an urgent 'turn-around' operation in any business. The *Telegraph* was in desperate financial straits; desperate action was needed. Financially, the scale of the turn-around was remarkable. A couple of years after the takeover the paper was well on the way to prosperity. In four years it was vastly profitable.

Just how much of this could be attributed to the editorial changes that were made? Hartwell, as Editor-in-Chief, had been planning editorial reforms scheduled to take place if only he could free his hands of the financial horror. Moreover, the real revolution that took place at that time in the British press was not a journalistic one, nor did it take place at the *Telegraph*'s art deco headquarters in Fleet Street. It happened down the river at Wapping, and the shot that was heard round the world was fired not by Conrad Black but by Rupert Murdoch, proprietor of *The Times* (and the *Sun*). Just a few weeks after the *Telegraph* takeover, Murdoch consummated his magnificently bold plot that got rid of the greedy printers overnight. The path to newspaper profitability lay wide open from that moment.

Meanwhile the most imaginative editorial innovation in 1986 was not taking place at the *Telegraph* but at the newly formed *Independent*. The fact that it was able to come into being proved that after a few years of Conservative government the basic rules of capitalism had reasserted themselves so as to make it much easier to raise capital to back an exciting new idea.

One way and another, 1986 was a year of revolution in British newspapers, revolution with strong Thatcherite overtones. In terms of political support, how did Thatcherism fare in the press changes?

Hastings, as we have seen, was not a Thatcherite Conservative, and was soon to be accused in some quarters of making the *Telegraph* take a 'wet' line on various issues – the Libyan bombings, which occurred shortly after he took over, for instance; or Ulster. Too much can be made of this. Bill Deedes had not really been a Thatcherite Conservative either. Neither had Hartwell. But the old *Telegraph* had certainly not been an organ that believed in rocking boats. The new *Telegraph* became more dashing, and even more determined not to be classified as the house magazine of the Tory party. The new *Independent* believed solidly in capitalism, but was not particularly enthusiastic about Mrs Thatcher. The same could be said, to some extent, of the *Financial Times*. So far as the quality press was concerned, Mrs Thatcher during her Premiership did not get the 100 per cent support she might have liked – if she had been a newspaper reader. She did much better with the tabloids. When the Conservatives won the 1992 election, Neil Kinnock – not usually the sort of man to blame the referee when his team gets beaten – went out of his way to lay much of the blame for his defeat at the door of the press.

Overall, Mrs Thatcher and her party got a good deal out of the press during the 1980s. And the press certainly got a good deal out of the Thatcher-backed assault on the print unions.

16

Once upon a time . . .

JEFFREY ARCHER

I CANNOT claim to know Jeffrey Archer well, but he did give me lunch at the Caprice in the halcyon days of his deputy-chairmanship of the Conservative party. Over the hors d'oeuvres he said, 'Julian, how much money do you think I pay each year in income tax?' He then told me. '£800,000, which is the combined salary of every cabinet minister.' Over the main course he told me the difference between being worth, say, ten million and fifteen: 'there is no difference'; while over the pud (the food at the Caprice is very good) he said, 'Norman and I understand each other. He knows that I know that he knows I am worth at least fifteen million pounds. Everyone knows Norman is worth only two thousand.' God, I wish I were as insecure.

The wealth of Jeffrey Archer is part of the folklore of the Thatcher years. He applied entrepreneurship to authorship. He wrote his way to prosperity from financial ruin in 1974. That was a year when the country too faced ruin, and the Tory party's solution lay in electing Margaret Thatcher as their leader. Getting the country out of the red took her rather longer than it took Jeffrey Archer to pay off his debts.

Does the one story tell us something about the other?

We have to start in the era that went before – the empty years, and the false hopes, of the Swinging Sixties, the years that saw the birth of designer culture, the period when we all assured ourselves that we had never had it so good.

In the early Sixties Jeffrey Archer was at Oxford, earning a Blue as a sprinter. When he became a household name, the profile writers, noting that the lad had been educated at Wellington and Oxford, sometimes added that Wellington was an appropriate school for the son of a military family. In fact the family's military connections are vague, and in any case it wasn't *that* Wellington to which he won a scholarship. He did indeed attend a public school, in Somerset, but it was less well known than the more famous one of the same name founded in memory of the Duke of Wellington in Berkshire.

Nor was his university career quite what it is usually thought. From school he had gone to America, where he trained as a PE teacher: he was an outstanding sprinter (who went on to run for Great Britain). He was frequently described as a young man in a hurry.

After teaching in an English public school he decided – being also an ambitious young man – that he ought to be at Oxford. He knew there was an Oxford Institute of Education whose diploma would add cachet. Unfortunately it was normally a post-graduate qualification, and he had no degree, but doors were opened by his athletic pre-eminence, his determination and his ability to impress his elders with his fresh-faced keenness. It was once said that he was the archetype of those notices one used to see in grocers' windows: 'Smart boy wanted'. In any case he found himself attached to Brasenose College.

These social niceties of his background are relevant. Jeffrey Archer's rapid rise as a Conservative politician – when he entered the Commons he was the youngest MP – then his fall, then his even more spectacular rise again, took place when the Tories were going through a social identity crisis.

They were questioning old assumptions about the importance of public schools, for instance, and military background. They were reassessing the balance to be struck in the ruling classes between 'old' families and self-made men, between gentlemanly amateurs and hard-nosed professionals. In the clubs and the Smoking Room at the Commons, Tories could sigh and tell themselves that in the old days things had been so simple. The country had been run by gents. Now the party had to come to terms with a new kind of gent . . . Perhaps it is no coincidence that they solved the problem, in a sense, by electing not a gentleman but a lady as their leader.

In the Sixties, Archer was characteristic of his generation in another way. He picked as his wife, interestingly, a career woman. He met Mary Archer (née Weeden) at Oxford. It seemed to be an attraction of opposites. He was the brash, extrovert athlete. She was a scholar, reserved and ladylike, an able and ambitious scientist who became, as a Cambridge don, an authority on solar energy.

Fame as an athlete, and finding the woman he loved – Jeffrey Archer had much for which to thank Oxford. At Oxford he developed a talent which provided the key to the next stage of his career. The brash, larger-than-life quality may have been tiresome to some of the stiffer elements at the university but was ideally suited for something else. Jeffrey found he could raise money for charity on a grand scale.

He inundated Oxford with Oxfam collecting boxes. The idea was that undergraduates could be exhorted or bullied into rattling them around the local pubs, but that was only to be part of the grandiose programme to raise half a million pounds. He signed on the Beatles. The public-schoolmaster in him may not have been instinctively in sympathy with Secondary Modern culture or Beatle-style haircuts, but he knew what the fans wanted. Ringo Starr was quoted as having remarked afterwards that 'that man would have bottled my pee and sold it'. Perhaps he did.

The Beatles were bidden to dine at High Table. The

Chancellor of the university, none other than Harold Macmillan, was persuaded to come too. As part of the hype, Archer jetted across the Atlantic and had an Oval Office interview with President Lyndon Johnson.

They raised only a quarter of a million, but that was impressive enough by any standard. The gimmickry of the campaign was duly recorded, indeed much of it had been inspired, by a local journalist called Nick Lloyd, who was destined for great things in Fleet Street but was then merely a 'stringer' in Oxford for various national papers.

Armed with this experience, an even larger measure of self-confidence, and now an instinct for playing along with the media, Archer arrived in London. Like politics, the world of charity fund-raising was going through a transformation in the Sixties. There too the amateur was being replaced by the professional. When Archer established an enterprise which promised to put a sharper edge on fund-raising, for a fee, he raised eyebrows – but he satisfied clients.

His sights were on loftier targets, however. As a first step in politics he became Tory Member for what had been a Labour seat on the Greater London Council – at the age of 27 its youngest member. In 1969 he entered the House of Commons at a by-election at Louth. His adoption was not entirely smooth – there were those who did not think he was a suitable person to become an MP.

He entered the House when Harold Wilson – another Sixties personality who made use of the Beatles – was then at the peak of his powers, but the greater part of Archer's brief parliamentary career was presided over by Heath. The sad story of the four years of the Heath government has been told often enough. It was a time when people were making (and then losing) fortunes in property. Archer was into property too – he tried, but failed, to take over Centre Point – but the investment that scuppered him was a Canadian industrial cleaning company called Aquablast. He was, to coin a phrase, taken to the cleaners, and lost £427,000. The threat of bankruptcy proceedings meant that continuance as an MP was unthinkable. He departed from Westminster just a few months before the start of the new era in Tory politics which was begun when Mrs Thatcher was elected Conservative party leader.

If Thatcherism meant anything, it had to do with people pulling themselves up by their own bootstraps. It took years for Archer to pay off his debts, but he did it, with exemplary determination. Thatcherism is also about a market economy ('You cannot buck the market'). Jeffrey raised the money he needed by using his talents to meet the demands of the marketplace.

His first book, *Not a Penny More, Not a Penny Less*, is a sort of parable of his own financial troubles. Four men are swindled by a City shark. They contrive an implausible scheme to trick the swindler out of precisely the amount of money he took from them – plus expenses. At the end the villain gets his come-uppance in a way that in an old-fashioned Hollywood movie would have had them cheering in the front stalls. It was a rattling good yarn, celebrating the triumph of morality over evil . . . Well, more precisely, the triumph of the rights of property.

An early draft of the novel was seen by an agent who correctly guessed its best-seller potential. The identity of the agent provided yet another link with the fast-moving political events of the time. She was Debbie Owen, wife of a leading Labour politician of the time called Dr David Owen, later to come under the influence of market economics himself and found his own party.

Not a Penny More, Not a Penny Less was a market triumph. Its natural appeal to the masses was notably enhanced by its author's grasp of the importance of publicity. (That was why, he liked to explain, he got to the top of the best-seller lists and Graham Greene didn't.) Over the years he evolved a technique that was the model of a market-orientated manufacturing process. Early drafts of his books were shown to a selection of ordinary people who were asked to mark sections they thought boring, so that these could be deleted, and to point to the characters they considered most robust, so that these could be expanded. Successive drafts were honed and refined. It was like the highly organized process whereby a car manufacturer develops a new model.

What of the books' literary merits? Archer was cheerfully modest about them. Critics acknowledged that the straightforwardness of his plots – like the plot of Jack and Jill, or the Three Bears – could hardly be faulted; but that the writing, by any acceptable literary standard, was appalling. For more sophisticated readers, the books were downright embarrassing because of the crudity of the method of creating background and atmosphere. Archer had walked the corridors of power, even if he did not fully grasp what went on there. He spelled out his memories with merciless efficiency, like an American tourist showing his neighbours his colour slides of a two-week vacation through fourteen capitals of Europe. And the name-dropping in Archer's books could be shameless. Politicians, royalty, show business stars stroll across the pages like celebrity guests at a TV chat show.

The formula made for compulsive reading. No sand-and-sun holiday on a Mediterranean beach during the Eighties was complete without a Jeffrey Archer paperback, stained with Ambre Solaire, to add to the feeling of complex relaxation. The very words 'a Jeffrey Archer' came to define a genre: the opium of the striving classes of the Thatcher years. The genre was unkindly summed up in a throwaway line in a book by another, rather different, Tory politician with literary ambitions: Douglas Hurd. In one of Hurd's stylish novels (*Palace of Enchantments*), a psychiatrist diagnoses a character as being dried up, and prescribes 'a course of intellectual hydration, say a Harold Robbins, or a Jeffrey Archer twice a month: when you have read them all, start again – you won't notice.'

By comparison with Harold Robbins, a typical Jeffrey

Archer is short on sex, but it is similar in being long on the pleasures of money, power and exotic environments. Small wonder that best-seller followed best-seller. Within them, character after character acquired fame and wealth and turned the tables on the forces that had once humiliated them.

It became increasingly difficult to differentiate between the fiction and the fact of the Jeffrey Archer lifestyle. He had acquired the Old Vicarage at Grantchester, famous (as he would have spelt it out in describing the home of one of his characters) as being the scene of the world-famous poem by the world-famous poet Rupert Brooke. As a town *pied-à-terre* he had a spectacular Thames-side penthouse (Henry Moore and Rodin among the conversation pieces) with a panoramic view over to the Houses of Parliament. He could look down on Westminster.

These details were freely available to gossip columnists. An *Observer* profile of the time noted Archer's accomplishment as a TV performer: 'Switch on a breakfast show and there he is, delivering his setpiece on the Romance of Authorship (which sounds like a lost chapter from *Scouting for Boys*)'. The same profile-writer noted his unique qualities as a dinner-table raconteur. 'The facts of the story are usually true (more or less) but they have been dismantled, new roles allocated, details dramatized as dialogue, and then reassembled again. It is, so to speak, the Cubist school of table-talk: the effect is striking but somewhat lacking in verisimilitude.'

Meanwhile, as the Archer phenomenon prospered, so did the Thatcher revolution in politics. A common factor was the importance of material wealth as a spur to endeavour. It was the age of the personalized car number plate. By 1985 it seems to have dawned on the Prime Minister that there was political mileage to be made by exploiting the parallel: the link between the cash nexus of the paperback plots of fiction and that of the enterprise society being acted out in the real Britain of the 1980s. Mrs Thatcher had now triumphed in two successive general elections. How could she make sure of a third victory? The troops needed rallying and fresh zest needed to be added to the message.

Archer was appointed deputy chairman of the Conservative party for the run-up to the election which was to take place in 1987. The then chairman of the party, Norman Tebbit, had his doubts. So, too, did Lord Whitelaw. It had been Mrs Thatcher's intention to send 'Jeffrey' to the Lords as Minister of Sport, but Willie would not wear it. So he went to Smith Square instead. In a matter of months, as Archer took on a punishing round of tours around the constituencies, eating ham salad and rubber chicken in draughty village halls, it was clear that he could scoop potential voters into the palm of his hand in the same way as he could potential readers.

He charmed audiences. Not with the smarm traditionally supposed to go down well with Tory old ladies. His style was nearer the cheeky chappie badinage of the street trader who has housewives giggling, 'Ooh, isn't he *awful*', and then digging into their purses. The charm was always tinged with an exciting bit of menace. One story told of a sporting occasion when he described a boy in the crowd as 'an odious little toad'; the parents were apparently delighted – their son had been noticed by the great man.

The story of Archer himself held its own fascination. Here was a man who had lost his father in his teens but had educated himself; there was the dramatic story of near-bankruptcy and the success story that followed; there were the evident trappings of the successful achiever, up at the crack of dawn, cold baths, hard games of squash. Audiences relished every word from his lips about the secret of the Thatcher enterprise society, about the need for people to stand on their own feet.

On political policy his touch was less certain. Comments on the situation in Northern Ireland had ministers coming out in a cold sweat. But there was no doubt that he brought in cash when the collecting box went round.

But Fate, as some novelists might say, had a nasty surprise waiting for Jeffrey Archer. Given the importance of the publicity factor in his life, the next part of the drama was full of irony.

As often happens with those who have provided journalists with excellent copy over the years, the attitude of the media to Jeffrey Archer was not one of unalloyed admiration. To put it bluntly, they were waiting to catch him out, and in 1986 they thought they had done it. In the event it was the media, not he, who had their come-uppance.

In the autumn of that year unproven stories were circulating in Fleet Street that a prostitute had identified Jeffrey Archer as one of her clients. The *News of the World* smelled an interesting little story, but held its hand to see if it could be made to turn from a minor into a major story. The prostitute was persuaded to phone Archer. He reacted with what he was shortly to acknowledge was great foolishness. Realizing, as he put it in a statement after the story broke, 'that for my part any publicity of this kind would be extremely harmful to me and for which a libel action would be no adequate remedy, I offered to pay her money so that she could go abroad for a short period'. He had been told that the woman wanted to escape hounding from the press.

A rendezvous was arranged. As in an Archer novel, the precise location was spelled out in detail in the published accounts – Platform 3 at Victoria Station. An emissary from Archer passed an envelope stuffed with £50 notes to the woman, under the eyes of a watching team from the *News of the World*, who duly printed their version of the story.

Archer had, in the words of his statement, allowed himself 'to fall into what I can only call a trap in which a newspaper, in my view, played a reprehensible part'. He had never met the woman and had never had any association with any prostitute, he declared, but 'for that lack of judgement, and that alone', he resigned as deputy chairman of the party.

He brought a libel action against the *News of the World*.

This was eventually settled out of court, but another action, against the *Star*, became a *cause célèbre*, and ended when a jury awarded a record sum of libel damages – £500,000 (which Jeffrey gave to charity).

The case spoke volumes about what jurymen think of the media, and about their view of how a newspaper must be punished if it libels a prominent man. They had heard quite a lot about newspaper methods. They had been told that journalists paid money to the prostitute while they persuaded her to approach Archer. They had listened while she herself in the witness box agreed that the offending *Star* article was largely 'sheer fantasy'.

The Archer libel case also spoke volumes about the feelings of the judge, Mr Justice Caulfield. 'You might have thought before this trial', he told the jury, 'that what you read in the newspaper is fact. Well, goodness, if you had such a thought, it must have disappeared from your minds long, long ago.'

The judge was at pains to convey to the jurors his deep respect for the demeanour of Mary Archer. 'Your vision of her probably will never disappear. Has she elegance? Has she fragrance? . . . Is she right when she says to you, you may think with delicacy, "Jeffrey and I lead a full life"?' It was indeed possible, the judge said, even for the happiest married man to seek adventures, but look at Mary Archer's husband. 'Is he in need of cold, unloving, rubber-insulated sex in a seedy hotel round about quarter to one on Tuesday morning?' The jury thought not.

The Eighties may have been the most media-conscious decade in history, and Jeffrey Archer was among those who understood that fact. But the media did not come out of the Archer libel action looking good. Even leaving aside what *The Times* called 'the partiality of the summing up', it would have been surprising if the press had emerged without a stain on its character; while Jeffrey Archer, looked at askance by the British establishment in the past, had the satisfaction of

160

knowing that when he submitted himself to the judgement of the ordinary citizens who sit on juries, he could win.

What is the real significance of his career? He was not a serious politician, but his story tells us much about the politics of the time. He was not a serious writer, but he tells us much about what people expect to find in their reading matter. The sorry tale of the libel case tells us much about what happens when the principle of 'giving the reader what he wants' goes over the top. Somewhere, there is surely a message here about the dangerously thin line that marks fact from fantasy?

Archer's footwork should command respect. Once Mrs Thatcher's Court Novelist, he survived her downfall to sign up with John Major. Mrs Thatcher wanted to send him to the Lords (at a second time of asking) but it was widely reported in the press that Lord Pym of the Scrutiny Committee had objected: but John succeeded where Margaret had twice failed; in June 1992 Archer at last became a Lord, proof, if ever it were needed, of Major's claim to build 'a classless society'.

17

The Auchtermuchty factor
SIR JOHN JUNOR

LIKE THE Roman legionaries, the New Model Army of Margaret Thatcher never succeeded in breaking into the Celtic fringe. To Thatcherite zealots, it was a mystery that Scottish voters had no time for Mrs Thatcher's party – did not many of her virtues derive from the same Protestant ethic of Scots from John Knox, through Adam Smith, down to all those dour Scottish accountants today who keep their eye on the bottom line of company balance sheets? Perhaps the explanation is that all the most Thatcherite Scots had actually come south, having decided shrewdly at an early age that their talents would be better appreciated outside their own country.

One Scot who got out early was John Junor. By the 1980s he was possibly the best-known Scotsman in England, writing a famous column that had millions of readers nodding their heads wisely and telling themselves that you have to hand it to old Junor – he knows how to sock it to them. He socked it to social workers and homosexuals, to intellectuals, to pompous old twits and miscellaneous other groups that the average Englishman longs to abuse but lacks the facility with words, not to mention the necessary bad taste, to do the job properly. He socked it to liberal-minded members of the Royal Family. As for politicians, he regarded Harold Macmillan as a poseur ('as phoney as a two-dollar bill') and Harold Wilson as spineless ('I doubted whether between his backstud and his backside there was anything but his braces').

He could be generous in his summing up of some politicians. 'Of all the people around Mrs Thatcher I have not the slightest doubt which one, in a perfect world, I would choose as her successor. Geoffrey Howe.' But it was his gift for homespun invective, developed into an art form, which seemed particularly appropriate to the Thatcherite years. The John Junor jolly brand of rudeness was one of the more disagreeable characteristics of public life in the 1980s.

His skill was to strike a chord with ordinary folk whose aspirations and prejudices lay in a misty past, remembered nostalgically. He had learned that skill at the feet of another worldly-wise Presbyterian given to nostalgia for the good old days, Lord Beaverbrook. Junor's view of the human condition was expressed in a folksy Scottish accent – it added to what may loosely be called his charm.

John Junor's father came from the Scottish Highlands, but he himself was born in Glasgow, in a tenement building in Maryhill. Years later, when he wanted to delight his readers with an idealized community possessed of all the homely Scottish virtues, he picked on the town of Auchtermuchty, which sounds fictional but is in fact an undistinguished place in Fife with little to commend it except the rhythmic banality of its name. After he started using its name, Junor liked to call in there when he went north from Fleet Street to play golf – Auchtermuchty is conveniently on the road to St Andrews. That seems to have been the extent of his understanding of its sociology, but the Auchtermuchty of his journalistic imagination warmed the heart of every honest *Sunday Express* reader. It was a place where the lassies were pretty, the lads were lusty, and there was short shrift for woofters and poofters.

It was typical of his journalistic talent to be able to create such a place. In fact Junor's original ambitions seem to have leant not towards journalism but towards politics, in which he had managed to give himself a sound grounding as a student at Glasgow University. That was just before the war. 'I was violently anti-Fascist, anti-Franco, above all anti-Hitler,' he wrote later. He was also instinctively anti-socialist. And although it was not a phrase he himself would have used, he was, above all, anti-Establishment. He joined the Liberal party.

In the Scottish Liberal circles of the pre-war world he made quite a hit. He became a valued young performer on the speaking circuit, and took a lively part in one important by-election when Chamberlain's Munich policy was the main issue. He enjoyed the opportunities to meet the local press. He also enjoyed contacts with the Scottish gentry.

When the summer of 1939 came, he found himself picked for the kind of mission most of us think of as taking place only in fiction. He was signed on (at the then not inconsiderable salary of £4 a week) by the fabulously rich and highly personable Lady Glen-Coats, a Liberal activist, as her private secretary to go on a fact-finding tour of Hitler's Germany. They were only just able to get a train out before the war started on 3 September.

Pre-war politics had been heady stuff for the boy from the Maryhill tenement. He developed a taste for moving among the mighty, and the world of well-laden tables and imaginatively stocked wine cellars. He came to enjoy being able to afford hand-made suits, and as a descriptive journalist he noted what kind of suits other people wore, just as he noted the wine they offered him.

The most characteristic setting for the mature John Junor was his favourite table in the Boulestin restaurant in Covent Garden, entertaining leading politicians. There he picked up and passed on gossip, and received whatever messages the politicians were anxious to convey to the greater public. His conversation, he liked to think, had a catalytic effect on policy-making at the top. These Boulestin meetings were the sort of occasion, one suspects, where each participant was convinced he was using the other. He developed reasonably close relations with a mixed bag of politicians. They included Quintin Hailsham, Reggie Maudling, Ted Heath (whose yachting enthusiasm was shared by Junor) and Manny Shinwell.

By the time Junor was holding court at the Boulestin he had been forced to give up, or at least to say that he had given up, his own political ambitions. He had unsuccessfully stood three times as a Liberal candidate. Beaverbrook had no prejudices against members of his staff who got involved in Liberal politics or similar eccentricities, but when he had earmarked somebody for a top job in his organization he made it clear that they had to choose: either politics or *Express* Newspapers.

Junor came to Beaverbrook's notice soon after the war, in which he served as a pilot. The latter stages of the war he spent editing the Fleet Air Arm's magazine, taking the opportunity to build up contacts in Fleet Street which stood him in good stead when he was demobilized. Before long he was on the *Daily Express*. 'I discovered early on that I would not have made a very good hard news reporter,' he writes in his memoirs. But he had the knack of writing about political personalities and was moved on to writing the 'Cross-Bencher' column in the *Sunday Express*. His proprietor liked what he read there, and Junor joined the select club of Beaverbrook cronies, liable to be called in to make up dinner parties or simply to produce or listen to ideas. He was even provided with a house on the Beaverbrook estate at Cherkley. In 1954 he became Editor of the *Sunday Express*.

Junor has since made it clear that he was well aware of the more disagreeable of his proprietor's qualities. There was the extraordinary episode which was arguably Junor's hour of glory. He had not long been Editor when he got into trouble with the Commons Committee of Privileges and was subject to the historic, but disagreeable, experience of being summoned to the Bar of the House to apologize. He did so in terms which defended the rights of the press in fairly robust terms.

Like many matters of parliamentary privilege, the episode looks in retrospect like a storm in a teacup. It occurred during the aftermath of the Suez crisis, when petrol was rationed. The *Sunday Express* published an editorial condemning MPs for getting 'prodigious supplementary allowances' of petrol while 'the small baker, unable to carry out his rounds, may be pushed out of business'. This was the true voice of Auchtermuchty, and one cannot help thinking that the Committee of Privileges in normal times might have been more relaxed about it. But nothing was normal in the frenetic politics of Suez. Moreover, if the committee's reaction was open to criticism, so was that of John Junor's boss. 'There was not a whisper of support from Lord Beaverbrook,' Junor writes of his ordeal in his memoirs. 'Whatever else he may have been, the old boy was no hero.'

Yet there was certainly a rapport between Junor and Beaverbrook. They shared the same view of politics in terms of colourful personalities. They were both political animals, although with no undue concern for consistency of political theory. The thinking of both men was rooted in a grandiose past which had probably never existed. In the 1950s Beaverbrook was preaching an unreconstructed imperialism which had no relevance in the post-war world and indeed little relevance in the pre-war one. By the time of Suez, such nostalgia was out of fashion with the educated classes and with the Establishment, but was by no means unattractive to voters for whom gut feelings are more important than political analysis. Beaverbrook and Junor may have been looked on askance by the Establishment, but they were able to carry ordinary newspaper readers with them.

Beaverbrook died before he was forced to face up to the failure of his vision of a patriotism that depended on Empire and on denying Britain's European dimension. Junor, forty years younger, adapted the same rugged patriotic individualism to the context of the late twentieth century. This made him one of the prophets of Thatcherism.

He edited the *Sunday Express* for a long time before he took over the column which made him his own most celebrated contributor. He started writing it, as it happens, at almost precisely the time that the Tory party chose Margaret Thatcher as its leader. He had met her for the first time just a few weeks before, during the frantic period in late 1974 when the party had decided that it wanted to get rid of Ted Heath but was unable to decide on a successor; few were predicting that the choice might fall on the Member for Finchley.

The initiative for that first meeting had come not from him but from her, or at least from her entourage. During the years before she became Prime Minister in 1979, those around Mrs Thatcher developed a shrewd view of her policy in regard to the media. They knew the quality press tended to be run by people who were not going to be easily won over to Thatcherism. It was the John Junors who could be won over.

Her public relations adviser, Gordon Reece, arranged a lunch with Junor – at the Boulestin. Junor regarded himself as a connoisseur of the Tory politicians of the time, and at that initial lunch meeting he did not find the future Tory leader over-impressive: in Auchtermuchty they preferred their politicians to be male. But it was not long before the Thatcher team seeking to woo Junor found that they were pushing at an open door. It came to him as a blinding light that what Auchtermuchty really wanted in that hour of the nation's need was the no-nonsense approach of a woman, a woman who believed in good housekeeping, a grocer's daughter who knew how to measure out the sugar.

It takes one to know one, and in Margaret Thatcher John

Junor recognized one of his own kind. At last the dream of his student days at Glasgow might come true. The Old Etonians and the effete Southerners who had run the country for so long were about to get their come-uppance. He was soon producing suggestions about how to purge the traditional Conservative party, and Mrs Thatcher was a willing pupil. Junor was an old hand at spotting weaknesses in the Establishment's armour. He was also good at suggesting names of other people she should recruit to the cause.

By a fairly early stage of the Thatcher Premiership Junor was able to claim with some justification that he was one of her real friends. She needed friends in those days. She had few in the Cabinet. She needed people she could talk to, in the confidence that they would not leak her weaknesses to her enemies. Junor knew about leaks, and he knew how they could be handled. It would be absurd to suggest that it was a shoulder to weep on: rather it was something for her to sharpen her sword on. John Junor proved a loyal friend. He was on the list for parties at Chequers. There were tête-à-têtes in Downing Street. And she became the greatest of the myriad of political guests at his luncheon table.

It seems unlikely that he ever made any substantive contribution to policy, or even that he provided her with any information that she could not have got elsewhere. But the Thatcherite revolution was not just a matter of policy. It was largely to do with ideas, and with expressing those ideas. That was where Auchtermuchty made a powerful contribution.

18

Nearer, my God, to Thee
RUPERT MURDOCH

THE LEFT has always been preoccupied by the political power of newspapers. The 'Tory press', like 'bloated capitalists', passed into the socialist mythology that the Labour party has only recently begun to question. Newspaper proprietors were supposed to twist the democratic process and prevent the honest working classes from claiming their rightful heritage. As often happens, the Left got it precisely the wrong way round: for about half of the twentieth century it was not the newspapers that screwed the working classes; it was working-class organization, refined by greedy print unions to a vicious mafia-type operation, that screwed the newspapers. For years, the printers used the closed shop to write their own pay cheques.

The mythology clouded the real nature of the relationship between capitalism and newspapers. In a free capitalist society, newspaper publishing can be extremely profitable. In accountancy jargon, newspapers are naturally strong generators of cash-flow. The public are happy to buy newspapers they enjoy, the advertisers are happy to pay large sums to advertise in newspapers that people buy.

A list of the press barons makes the point. Lord Northcliffe built up a fortune, a hundred years ago, by founding the *Daily Mail* when he saw that there was money to be made out of the first generation of the English working classes to be compulsorily taught to read and write. He ended mad, and he had strong political views that found their way into the columns of his papers – but making money was really what it was all about. Lord Beaverbrook always boasted that his motivation in running the *Daily Express* was to promote his political ideas, not to make profits – but who remembers his quirky political notions today? Yet his skill in identifying a profitable readership remains an example to the publishing industry. That other giant of Fleet Street between the wars, Lord Camrose, proved, by building up the *Daily Telegraph*, that there was a profitable market to be exploited in the characteristic English middle class's ethos of the 1930s: it was its conservatism with a small c rather than its Conservatism that was the key.

Of course there have been the altruists. The Quaker Cadburys were willing to sink money in the old *News Chronicle*, and the saintly Lord Astor was prepared to use his fortune to foster high-minded journalism in the *Observer*. But the newspaper proprietor who described his own motives in the most engaging way was Roy Thomson, who made no secret of his delight (when he expanded from newspapers into television) at having found a 'licence to print money'. Thomson (like Beaverbrook) was a Canadian, and bluff colonials have a way of cutting through to basics. The Australian influence in newspaper tycoonery was still to come.

Rupert Murdoch appeared in Fleet Street in the late 1960s. The initial reaction was predictably patronizing: Fleet Street knew all about Australians – they were those rough characters who were to be seen down the Earls Court Road, swilling beer, and there was a sort of beer-swilling image to the paper selected for the first Murdoch acquisition: the *News of the World*. This Sunday paper, which Murdoch shrewdly identified as being ripe for change, liked to regard itself as a fine old English institution; others saw it simply as a paper for dirty old men, and it was hard to summon up much patriotic indignation at a new proprietor who planned to throw its tradition out of the window. Perceptive people in Fleet Street wondered whether Murdoch perhaps represented an interesting breath of fresh air on the London scene.

In any case, it was difficult to dismiss him as a mere roughneck from the outback. Keith Rupert Murdoch was educated at Geelong Grammar School ('the Australian Eton') and Worcester College, Oxford. His father, Sir Keith Murdoch, was a distinguished and courageous war correspondent – he helped to expose the scandal of the Gallipoli campaign in the First World War – who became an editor and then a publisher (and was nearly brought to London to edit *The Times*). Rupert's mother, Dame Elisabeth, acquired a title of her own. The young Rupert grew up in an atmosphere which made him feel at home among journalists, businessmen and politicians. He was only 21 when his father died. As with many men in a hurry, a motivating force in Murdoch's life was apparently to do all the things his father had left undone.

While still a young man he built up a substantial Australian media empire by following some fairly simple principles. One was to give the public what they wanted, rather than what the great and the good of this world think people *ought* to want. This application of lusty free-market economics was in due course to be brought to England and carried to a high point in the *Sun*. Another Murdoch principle was that running newspapers is a rough old business; in other words, not to put too fine a point on it, he acquired a reputation for ruthlessness.

A third important principle was to keep control of his companies in his own hands as far as possible. He was chary about spreading equity shares. He had none of the distaste, still to be found in the more old-fashioned British businessman, for operating with a lot of debt, and he was adept at reaching deals with banks to finance his acquisition programmes. But of course you cannot cope with debt unless you have ample cash-flow, in order to service the debt. Hence – and this was something Murdoch executives and Murdoch editors ignored at their peril – his papers had to make money.

When he established himself in London as proprietor of the *News of the World*, he had enough experience in Australian publishing to regard himself as a seasoned professional in the newspaper trade – very much more professional than some people in high positions in Fleet Street. Among Fleet Street dailies on the sick-list at that time was the paper which had once been the Labour party's *Daily Herald*. It was now owned by the *Mirror* Group, where that old Fleet Street magician Hugh Cudlipp had tried to breathe some modern version of left-wing fervour into it without success, although – to symbolize a new dawn – it had been given a new name: the *Sun*. The title was now for sale – for £50,000 cash down.

In 1969 Murdoch bought it. As editor he selected Larry Lamb (who was in due course to feature in one of Mrs Thatcher's earliest honours lists as Sir Larry). The 'soaraway *Sun*' became part of the history of the 1970s.

The 1970s was not the happiest of decades. It began with the high hopes, and then the sad disappointments, of Ted Heath's administration. It was the decade which saw the striking miners pushing Ted Heath out of Downing Street and bringing back Harold Wilson, and then the Tories replacing Ted with Margaret. All these events were recorded in the columns of the new Murdoch-owned *Sun* – although, it is fair to say, not at any great length. Other parts of the paper were occupied by matters of a less serious kind.

It was a new kind of newspaper. 'Page 3' took on a special meaning which outraged the feminists of the 1970s but clearly gave horny-handed working men pleasure which they had never got from the worthy pages of the old *Daily Herald*.

But of course, it was not just indelicate photographs that caused the *Sun* to soar upwards as it did. The real indelicacy lay in the whole editorial approach. It was to be a paper that cocked a snook at the respectable way of doing things. At a time when the great and the good were talking about being nice to Europeans, the *Sun* could come out with a headline telling the Frogs to 'hop it'. In the solemnity of the Falklands War, it could greet the sinking of the *Belgrano* with the celebrated headline 'Gotcha!' The *Sun* didn't like foreigners, it didn't like social security scroungers and it didn't like gays. As it developed its robust character during the 1970s, it outraged the civilized middle classes. But then, Murdoch, like many another Australian, had never had much time for the self-proclaimed civilized middle classes of the old country. He wasn't publishing a newspaper for them. He knew that his headline writers had caught the authentic voice of the man in the pub.

The *Sun* was an anti-Establishment paper. In other words, it was going to fill the role that the *Daily Mirror*, in its heyday, had played when it was the cheeky urchin of Fleet Street, able to cause Winston Churchill, among others, to lose his temper. The great difference was of course that the *Mirror* had been left-wing; the *Sun* was on the right.

That brings us to Rupert Murdoch's personal politics. At Oxford he is said to have been known as 'Red Rupert', active in the Labour Club (but banned from it for canvassing for office). He was sufficiently 'Australian' to be irritated by traditional British Conservative assumptions of superiority. Larry Lamb, who had ample opportunity to observe the proprietor of the *Sun*, put it thus:

> He was obsessed, to what I sometimes regarded as an alarming degree, by what he chose to call the 'English' class system. It was futile to point out that class systems based upon race and income, as in most of the United States, and most of Australia, are often more pernicious than those based upon ancestry.

The British monarchy is the pinnacle of the 'English class system'. Murdoch makes no secret of his republican sympathies.

The *Sun* and the *Sunday Times* between them (with a little help from the *Mail*) threaten to bring the Royals into disrepute.

As an Australian newspaper proprietor, Murdoch had supported the Labour party of Gough Whitlam in the election campaign of 1972 but then turned against him, and his papers played an important role in the constitutional controversy when the Governor-General dismissed Whitlam.

When it came to British politics, there was little doubt in Murdoch's mind about the direction the *Sun* had to follow in the mid-1970s. If he was going to produce a cheeky, anti-Establishment paper, there was no point in following the disintegrating Labour party under its Byzantine leader, Harold Wilson. The politician to watch was Margaret Thatcher. It was not just that she was in sympathy with swash-buckling Murdoch-style capitalism. The new proprietor of the *Sun* saw, as the majority of Conservatives probably did not, what Mrs Thatcher was doing in the years between her election as party leader in 1975 and her arrival in Downing Street four years later. She was detaching herself from the Establishment and devising a political philosophy with a 'classless' appeal. Specifically it would appeal to a wide section of what used to be called the working class which had traditionally looked to the Labour party as serving its interests.

Those close to Mrs Thatcher in the run-up to the 1979 election saw that there was little mileage to be made in wooing the quality press: quality journalists were instinctively patronizing, if not downright hostile, towards the Tories' new leader. The grander of them regarded themselves as being among the great and the good, whom Mrs Thatcher despised. So her public relations advisers told her, in effect: forget the posh papers and the posh TV and radio programmes; get on the Jimmy Young Show, and cultivate the *Express*, the *Mail* and Murdoch's brash new *Sun*.

The relationship worked both ways. For a time, the *Sun*'s columnists included, of all people, Mrs Thatcher's guru Sir Keith Joseph, explaining his austere market-economy philosophy in words of few syllables. But the more important influence of the *Sun* in changing the philosophy of the nation lay not so much in overt politics as in its attitude to everything it covered. There was nothing to be ashamed of (it seemed to shout at its readers) in looking at titillating pictures of nude girls. Equally, there was nothing to be ashamed of in enjoying titillating snippets of scandal, even if the facts had to be massaged a little to make the story more interesting. Voyeurism on a national scale was on tap for a few pennies per copy. Give the punters what they paid for. In this way, while Mrs Thatcher was preaching the virtues of a free society, the *Sun* was practising its own kind of freedom from constraints.

In commercial terms, the formula worked superbly. The moribund paper that Murdoch had bought for a pittance had had a circulation in 1969 of something like 650,000. By 1978 it had topped the 4 million mark, the best-selling paper in Britain. Even though it was still being produced by old technology, manned by absurdly over-paid print workers, it was making a fortune for its proprietor, who was able to continue building his world empire, acquiring the *New York Post* in 1979 and going on to acquire television and film interests.

By now Murdoch was settled into a jet-age lifestyle, his office a briefcase open on his knee in a pressurized cabin miles above one or other of the world's oceans. His interest in the British scene was undiminished, however.

When the 1979 election came, the *Sun*, not noted for publishing long texts, addressed its readers on election day in a leading article that covered three pages. Today, it proclaimed, was 'the first day of the rest of our lives'. The editorial, directed particularly at 'traditional supporters of the Labour party', concluded: 'Vote Tory. Stop the Rot. There may not be another chance.'

Larry Lamb has put it on record that his boss had 'significant reservations' about the article, and tinkered with the wording. But it marked Murdoch's entry into the new, Thatcherite establishment. There was every reason for Mrs

Thatcher to be grateful to him for creating this new paper of the 1970s. As Larry Lamb, in his memoirs, *Sunrise*, explains:

> The *Sun*, addressing itself to an essentially working-class audience of around 13 million, was probably talking to most of the people who could be persuaded to switch their political allegiance . . . Elections are sometimes won or lost on swings of only 1 or 2 per cent. If the *Sun* succeeded in convincing only 1 or 2 per cent of its vast readership that a vote for the Tories was the only way to stop the rot, then the influence could have been critical, if not decisive.

Whether for that reason or not, enough working-class people did switch their allegiance in the 1979 election. And after it, during the next few years, when unemployment soared, it was invaluable for the government to have the sympathy of a working-class paper that believed in the aims of the Thatcher revolution. When a great celebratory lunch was held to mark ten years of Mrs Thatcher in office, Murdoch was among the ten guests at the Prime Minister's table. In the meantime Murdoch had brought about his own revolution, which was itself a major contribution to Thatcherism: Wapping.

In 1981 he made the most high-profile acquisition of his career: he bought *The Times* and the *Sunday Times*, which had got into a parlous financial condition. For the master of tabloid newspaper publishing, it was a bold move – and to much of the thinking British public a frightening move. The acquisition was not referred to the Monopolies Commission, on the ground that no other viable future for the papers was apparent. Murdoch's wife was quoted as saying of this latest takeover that it was 'not something I really want, but if Rupert wants it and it makes him happy, I'm sure we'll sort it out'. Some of the fears that *The Times* would slide down-market proved to be exaggerated. But the days when it was an institution rather than a newspaper had clearly come to an end.

Murdoch now owned a formidable slice of what was in those days still called Fleet Street – an industry operating with basically Victorian technology and with a labour force that could and frequently did make crippling demands on newspaper proprietors. The reforms introduced by the Thatcher government to reduce the special legal privileges of trade unions in industrial disputes had done little to tame the Fleet Street unions. It was Murdoch, in 1986, who tamed them. He simply moved his papers to a new printing works behind barbed wire at Wapping, and some five thousand trade unionists at the old establishments found themselves out of a job, because their work was now being carried out, more efficiently, by a much less costly workforce who belonged either to no union or to one (the electricians') which was prepared to deal with Murdoch on his new terms.

It was perhaps the greatest single victory in the long, messy war that has been waged between Britain's trade unionists and their employers. The reaction of organized labour to Murdoch as a person was explosive but powerless. Where Mrs Thatcher was merely extremely unpopular with trade union militants, it was Murdoch who was suddenly elevated to the role of Beelzebub in Labour demonology.

For months the pickets at Wapping seethed outside the tall steel gates defended by Murdoch's security men. His new workforce were ferried in in buses, with steel mesh over the windows, which picked them up at secret rendezvous points around London. There were pitched battles between pickets and police. There was near-apoplexy on the Opposition benches in the Commons about this colonial who had dared to stand against the god-given privileges of unionized print workers.

But at the end of the day the brash Australian did what countless British employers had only been able to dream of doing for years – raising two fingers at organized labour and getting away with it. It was a victory to stand alongside the defeat of Arthur Scargill's miners.

The Wapping victory gives Murdoch an honoured place in

the pantheon of Thatcherism. So does the *Sun*, which tells us more than Thatcherites might like to think about the instincts they are appealing to. Mrs Thatcher certainly felt that he had a rapport with the British people that paralleled hers. If he had been a Beaverbrook, with political aspirations, who knows what tasks she might not have found for him to do in the public domain? There are several reasons why Murdoch would not have been tempted. He clearly prefers making money. And basically he always seems to have had a healthy contempt for politics and politicians. Moreover, he formally disqualified himself from taking a more active role in British life when he became an American citizen: US law requires that US TV stations must be owned by Americans. And owning TV stations has always meant a lot to him.

Rupert Murdoch went into Sky Television and got God at more or less the same time. His religious conversion has received little publicity and could well have happened, if it did at all, on the road to Damascus, Illinois. I should admit that there is as yet no sign of his editorial influence being exercised upon his newspapers in matters pertaining to religion. In a nation of *Sun* worshippers there can be some room for faith, little for hope and none whatever for charity. Nevertheless, there must be rejoicing in heaven.

The deity might well, on the other hand, resent having to share His space with Sky television, whose plastic satellite dishes have become the badge of the British working class. In May 1992 there was an announcement that, at long last, the network, which had previously absorbed its rival, BSB, was 'operating at a profit'. I doubt if even Rupert Murdoch himself, who had spent the better part of the previous two years 're-scheduling his debts', yet knows how great were the original losses. Murdoch used, whenever he visited London, to pay a call upon Mrs Thatcher, but times have changed. The 'dirty digger', as *Private Eye* so unkindly calls him, has yet to take tea with her successor. Mr Major has a shorter set of spoons.

19

Man overboard

ROBERT MAXWELL

ROBERT MAXWELL was the bad taste left in the mouth after the 1980s. And, as always when we are left with a nasty taste on the morning after, there was no excuse for it. The definitive summing up of Maxwell had been delivered as far back as 1971, by a Department of Trade and Industry report in words that rang from Threadneedle Street to Carey Street:

> We regret having to conclude that, notwithstanding Mr Maxwell's acknowledged abilities and energy, he is not in our opinion a person who can be relied on to exercise proper stewardship of a publicly quoted company.

The 1971 DTI report, at a time when Britain's financial community was going through one of its phases of merger mania, had been a great moment of truth, a moment of rare clarity in the rhetoric of the City of London. It was the gentlemanly equivalent of the authorities putting Maxwell up against a wall, shooting him through the head and, for good measure, driving a stake through his heart. Never again . . .

Never again, that is, until the Enterprise Eighties. In the

Eighties it was a question of who dared, could win. Robert Maxwell, boy escapee from the Nazis in Czechoslovakia in 1939 and Second World War winner of a Military Cross, was nothing if not daring. The 1980s saw him born again. He emerged as one of the corporate giants of the enterprise years, a commercial colossus straddling not only both sides of the Atlantic but also both western and eastern Europe.

Then, when the Eighties had ended, his empire collapsed yet again, for very much the same reasons that had occasioned the DTI denunciation twenty years earlier. His final downfall was likewise on the scale of a colossus. When he was revealed as a cheat and a chancer, a robber of the savings of his company pensioners, the repercussions went far beyond the boundaries of the vast, complex Maxwell commercial network. The bankers, the Stock Exchange, all the pundits of the City of London who still operated, even in these cynical days, on the basis of a man's word being his bond, had to go back to the drawing board. Yet again the City establishment was left with a scarlet face, even more embarrassed than the Leftist establishment which had had to take him into its fold when he was a Labour MP.

Robert Maxwell and Rupert Murdoch were the two high-profile newspaper tycoons of their day. They fought for the same market, bidding for the same newspaper titles when they came up for sale. (It tended to be Murdoch who always pipped Maxwell at the post.) They were both tough operators, it went without saying. There were other superficial similarities. They were both parvenus on the British scene, underestimated by the old guard. In that sense, they were both made for the Enterprise Eighties.

But there was all the difference in the world between the Aussie parvenu Murdoch, who had been born with an Australian silver spoon in his mouth, and the former Jan Ludvik Hoch, born of Jewish peasant stock on the borders of Romania, who had had to go barefoot in childhood. Jan Hoch's adoption of socialism when he appeared on the British scene as Ian Robert Maxwell was the genuine reaction of an underdog, although the parliamentary Labour party was never easy with it: he was a millionaire by the time he got to Westminster. Rupert Murdoch's fairly brief adherence to the Labour party smacked more of champagne socialism.

Jan Ludvik/Ian Robert rose from poverty to riches by his wits – his 'acknowledged abilities and energy', in the words of the DTI report. The acknowledgement really began during the war when he was accepted for a commission in the British Army. As Captain Maxwell he became involved with military intelligence because of his linguistic aptitude. He had nine languages. How far he was ever drawn into the darker arts of the intelligence world was one of the tantalizing secrets he took with him to his watery grave.

He stuck with the title 'Captain' long after most wartime officers reverted to being plain 'Mister'. He seemed to need the trappings of authority to give him confidence. The most characteristic picture of Maxwell is of a huge man behind a huge desk which would still seemed dwarfed by his enormous bulk. And the telephones on the desk were all-important props – visitors would find the conversation interrupted at a crucial moment by the great man taking a call, supposedly, or sometimes actually, from a Cabinet minister or from the president of the latest country where he had struck a deal to gain a foothold for the Maxwell trading operation.

Early on in his career as an entrepreneur he calculated that it was important to have a chauffeur – that way, he explained, he could usefully employ the time spent on his way to meetings to work out his negotiating tactics. That at least rang true. His skill in dominating meetings was formidable. To the end he was able, for instance, to chair a meeting of the trustees of his employees' pension fund and persuade them, by a mixture of charm, bombast and the sheer brutality of the bully boy, that they had no right to doubt that their money was being lovingly cared for.

His business career took shape in the sad, grey John Le

Carré-like Central Europe of the immediate post-war period. The skill of being able to deal with foreigners in their own languages was sufficiently rare among British Army officers to make him a natural to work in the military government of Allied-occupied Europe. He was put in charge of supervising the rebirth of newspapers in Berlin, and according to one story would solemnly 'press the button for democracy' at 3 a.m. every morning to start the presses of *Die Telegraf.*

Running a newspaper – running any kind of business in post-war Berlin – was a nightmare. The necessary materials had to be sought out and bargained for, licences had to be negotiated from the authorities. It was the kind of challenge Maxwell relished. Corners were there only to be cut. He was a good man to have on your side when deals were being made: people on the other side of the deal were often less attracted to the young Captain Maxwell.

He retained his German contacts after being demobbed and setting up his first company in London. By that time he knew what he wanted, which was to be a millionaire.

He was willing to deal in anything, in those days of constant shortages, but soon focused on a commodity that he saw, shrewdly, was going to be more in demand than anything: knowledge. Post-war Europe was hungry for books, particularly scientific books and journals. By the early 1950s he had established himself in an ex-bottling plant in Marylebone Road, staffed by a motley of *émigrés* and refugees, full of books stacked among the old bottling machines. The same building housed his various other deal-making activities: Maxwell's Bazaar, somebody called it. At one time he was setting up complex barter deals involving pork bellies and prefabricated houses.

He was now running several supposedly separate companies, but was already adept at inter-company deals which remained a feature of his business methods ever after. One device was to 'sell' books from one company to another, and record the profits in the accounts. But there could be an agreement that the buying company had the right to return the books. It was an arrangement which made it much easier to balance accounts all round. Another characteristic of even the earliest network of Maxwell companies was that the financial threads led back to a family trust set up in Liechtenstein.

Gradually his interest focused on one of his companies, called Pergamon. The Pergamon Press was to be built into an internationally respected publisher of scientific books and journals, with a carefully structured motto, *Invanimus viam aut faciemus* – 'We shall find a way or we shall make one'. Nobody could claim that they had not been warned.

The academic world, on the whole, seemed to think Pergamon was a Good Thing – even if they thought it would be nice if it brought its prices down, and even if his learned authors sometimes grumbled about the level of the fees Maxwell paid them.

The knowledge market boomed. Britain was on the threshold of the Robbins revolution. With the advent of the plate-glass universities, the size of the academic population exploded. Maxwell was now a very rich man. The next step was to get into politics.

His devoted secretary is on record as explaining why he became a Labour MP by saying simply that 'The Tories wouldn't have had him'. Certainly Harold Macmillan, Conservative Prime Minister of the day, had no high regard for Maxwell. Harold was a publisher too, of a rather different kind. The publishing fraternity, then still supposed to be run by gentlemen, tended to look down their collective noses at Maxwell as he churned out profits, but they were not always averse to doing business with him. Harold, before he became Prime Minister, once complained that his firm had 'lost a fortune' in a complicated commercial arrangement which had left Macmillan's as creditors of one of the Maxwell companies which went into receivership.

In any event, it was Labour that got the benefit of the

Maxwell political talents. His zeal was unquestionable, to start with anyhow. As MP for Buckingham, he made the very first maiden speech of the new Parliament elected in the general election of 1964. As was remarked at the time, we could be grateful that at least he waited for the Queen to finish her speech before he started his.

As an orator, Maxwell made up with aplomb for what may have been lacking in depth of intellectual content. Soon he was active in the long-forgotten 'I'm backing Britain' campaign. The Harold Wilson regime did not, to his annoyance, offer him a ministerial appointment. Instead, it was decided that his talents could be usefully employed as Chairman of the Catering Committee, with a brief to reduce the loss on the House's various catering activities. He threw himself into the job and made the department show a profit, although only over protests from Members who complained about everything from the disappearance of *oeuf en gelée* to the deterioration of the quality of the biscuits in the tea-room. Later, however, the critics were asking whether it was really a profit after all? For one thing, Maxwell had arranged for a Treasury grant to underwrite the operation. He had also – and there are some who have never forgiven him for this – sold the wine cellar. Yet another omen of what was to come.

Wealth, a voice in the corridors of power at Westminster – what next? Maxwell's ambition for years had been to move into newspaper publishing. He spotted the opportunity to take over the *Sun* (in the event to be taken over by Murdoch). To raise the money he negotiated to sell Pergamon to an American organization. This was the deal which led to denunciation by the DTI inquiry. Briefly, he had presented the company as being much more profitable than it was. This was done by manipulation of the dealings between his various companies and exaggerating the levels of sales. Grisly stories emerged of sets of encyclopaedias mouldering unsold although their value had gone through the sales ledgers.

There followed years of bickering which seemed to reduce

186

Maxwell to an unpleasant memory. But that was to underestimate the resilience of the Bouncing Czech. By the time the 1980s came, he was bidding for one of Britain's major media groups, the British Printing Corporation.

The arrival of the Enterprise Eighties was a time for tearing away restrictions that had been condemned by businessmen in the past for preventing them from doing what they wanted to do. At long last the trade unions were beginning to be brought to heel. Then again, the barriers on switching funds from one country to another were being pulled down – the British were now to compete in a global market. And financial mechanics were liberalized in ways which made it easier to put together deals on the basis of large amounts of debt. Robert Maxwell was among those who made ample use of all these features of the enterprise economy.

At BPC – which suffered like all big printing houses of the time from the greed of the printing workforce – he took a robust stand against the unions and got away with it. This was years before Rupert Murdoch's Wapping revolution and Maxwell deserves credit for it.

His business had always been international, but now he forged ahead with ever more ambitious schemes to create a world 'communications' empire. He took over the American publishing operations of the Macmillans and the New York *Daily News*. He moved into France. And at home his dream of owning a major British newspaper came true when he was able to take over the *Daily Mirror*. He went on to found two new papers, the ill-starred *London Daily News* and the *European*.

His personal lifestyle was on a scale to match his imperial ambitions. He bought, for about £45 million, the yacht which he named after his daughter, the *Lady Ghislaine*. To celebrate his sixty-fifth birthday he spent an estimated quarter of a million pounds on entertaining 3,500 guests at his mansion in Oxford. Each guest received a copy of the recently published 'authorized biography' of their host. The story of the publication of that biography itself told much about the man. It was commissioned specifically to counter an unauthorized book which Maxwell went to elaborate pains to try to suppress. Like some other Maxwell publications, the authorized biography sold less well than he had hoped – the gifts at the Oxford party were yet another example of the characteristic Maxwell method of keeping the figures up.

In his relations with journalists he could behave like a parody of the megalomaniac newspaper tycoons of fiction. The biographer whose work he tried to suppress, Tom Bower, records in *Maxwell: The Outsider* how he interfered with the *Mirror* Editor's treatment of news in the last days of the Soviet empire. When told of the invasion of Lithuania, Maxwell responded, according to Bower: 'Nonsense. Don't you realize that Gorbachev wouldn't do anything without ringing me first?'

His own empire was crumbling as fast as Gorbachev's. The level of debts was now mountainous. Maxwell was not alone among entrepreneurs of the late 1980s in finding himself massively overgeared financially and reeling under the burden of high interest rates, but none had such a vast burden. He had raised much of the debt on the security of the shares of his companies, and the value of those shares had been kept up only on the basis of information which now seemed increasingly questionable.

Many British businesses were confronted by a moment of truth at the end of the 1980s. None was on such a grotesque scale as the truth facing Maxwell when he went off for his last holiday aboard the *Lady Ghislaine*. His very last debt, on his last evening alive, was when he borrowed a thousand pesetas from one of the crew to tip the taxi driver who had taken him for a lonely night out on the town in Santa Cruz. A few hours later, he was dead. A month later the Fraud Squad had been called in.